Praise for
Working Families

"Refreshing for its social conscience…sharp humor, and snappy prose. One of the more thoughtful guides to Christian family life for the twenty-first century."
—*Publisher's Weekly*

"…a joyous, wide-eyed ride on the roller coaster that is a strong marriage with kids!"
—MARCUS HUMMON, Grammy-award winning songwriter
of No. 1 hits including "God Bless the Broken Road"

"To know one's calling is a complex business—especially for women and men who are trying to keep integrity as wives and husbands, parents, professionals, and global citizens—all within the context of finding our way as pilgrims in pursuit of God. *Working Families* is an unusually wise book, pointing us in the right direction, and Joy Jordan-Lake is a gifted writer and skillful guide, inviting us to smile even as she leads us into the most important questions about who we are and what we do."
—STEVEN GARBER, author of *The Fabric of Faithfulness* and director
of The Washington Institute for Faith, Vocation, & Culture

"With great wit and honesty, Jordan-Lake addresses here the most urgent question confronting America today: *How now, Lord, shall we live?* Only one who has wrestled repeatedly with that question could tell this story at all, and only a very gifted writer could tell it this well."
—PHYLLIS TICKLE, author of more than two dozen books, including
her latest, *The Night Offices,* and The Divine Hours series

"Who says you can't have it all? Joy Jordan-Lake's *Working Families* is an often humorous but mainly bottom-line look at the joys and frustrations, the bonuses and the sacrifices of two-parent/two-career homes. Using her experience with sailing (and you'll have to read the book to know what that's about!), Jordan-Lake blesses her readers with applicable solutions for the reality of it all."
—EVA MARIE EVERSON, author of *Oasis* and The Potluck Club series

"Jordon-Lake defuses the grenades of guilt we lobby at other women and ourselves. She reminds us of the awesome accountability we have to use our professional gifts as well as to love and nurture our families. Her beautiful writing and often-hilarious stories remind me to be grateful for the chaos as well as the peaceful moments in family life. I felt encouraged and understood—and only wish I had this book ten years ago."

—CINDY CROSBY, author of *By Willoway Brook*

"Having sailed my way through a three-career family without a map, I'm delighted to know my daughter-in-law and others currently on the journey have a wonderfully, humorously, sensibly written work from which to take heart. Joy Jordan-Lake's experiences of trying to have it all are honest and exactly where the boat meets the water. Chaos may abound, flexibility must reign, and communication is essential, but swapping out a mindset about how things are supposed to be with the creativity of what can be is a trade worth making for men, women, and their fortunate children. Wisely, Jordan-Lake is on course with her conclusion that it's not a complete map that's needed but evaluating honestly what's in front and doing your best with God's help."

—MARY ANN MAYO, author of fourteen books,
including *Twilight Travels with Mother*

"Joy Jordan-Lake has written a delightful book full of challenge. Focusing on calling, purpose, and work, she shows us how to take God seriously in all arenas of life. Her "Navigating by Grace" chapter is more than just a catchy title. There's wisdom here for all of us in our daily work."

—HOWARD E. BUTT JR., author of *The High Calling of Our
Daily Work* and president of Laity Renewal Foundation

Working Families

Navigating the Demands and Delights of Marriage, Parenting, and Career

Joy Jordan-Lake

WATERBROOK
PRESS

WORKING FAMILIES
PUBLISHED BY WATERBROOK PRESS
12265 Oracle Boulevard, Suite 200
Colorado Springs, Colorado 80921
A division of Random House Inc.

ISBN 978-0-87788-199-5

Library of Congress Cataloging-in-Publication Data
Jordan-Lake, Joy, 1963-
    Working families : navigating the demands and delights of marriage, parenting, and career /Joy
Jordan-Lake. —1st ed.
        p. cm.
    Includes bibliographical references.
    ISBN-13: 978-0-87788-199-5
  1. Family—Religious aspects—Christianity. 2. Work and family. 3. Dual-career families. I. Title.
    BT707.7.J67 2007
    248.4—dc22

                                    2006031683

Printed in the United States of America
2007—First Edition

10 9 8 7 6 5 4 3 2 1

For the love of my life,
Todd Lake,
my co-parent and co-worker and dearest, best friend
and
for the three most magnificent kids imaginable,
our Jasmine, Justin, and Julia.

How grateful to God I am for you
for every hour of every day.

Contents

Acknowledgments

I t's only right that the first name on this particular page should be Elisa Stanford, the person who, as the acquisitions editor, was the initial champion for this book, and who later became its working-from-home editor. A mother and a writer herself, Elisa was unfailingly insightful, both from a personal and professional perspective. Her level-headed expertise and keen eye kept this book on track and alive. I am grateful for her hard work and her friendship.

When Thanne Moore ransacked her own bookshelves for books not to loan but to give me on the subjects of child-rearing and professional calling, I promised to place her way toward the top of the acknowledgments page, and, Thanne, here it is. You are marvelous.

It was Gloria and Ray White Hammond, medical doctors and African Methodist Episcopal ministers, who set aside their cell phones—the first in the neighborhood back then—to counsel Todd and me over a Formica-topped kitchen table before our marriage. They then set aside their good Yankee sense to travel more than a thousand miles into a small, white, southern town in deepest Dixie to officiate our wedding. For many of us, they have set an example of what a dynamic three-career marriage and what a journey of faith, including sacrifice and risk and vulnerability, might look like.

To those who, out of time they did not have, granted interviews, some in person and some via email or phone, I owe my everlasting and enthusiastic thanks: Doris Betts, Dawn Carlson, Elaine Chao, Shannon Sedgwick Davis, Diana Garland, Jennifer Grant, Andria Hall, Ray Hammond, Robin Hanna, Joe Kickasola, Linnea Kickasola, Bruce Kuhn, Susan Bahner Lancaster, Linda Livingstone, Mairead Corrigan Maguire, Susan Matthews, Vashti Murphy McKenzie, Thanne Moore, Carole Pomilio, Elizabeth Rogers, Kelly Shushock, Jane Tan, Ching-hua Tseng, Sally Weaver, Peggy Wehmeyer, Gloria White-Hammond, Patricia Wilson, Karla Worley.

And to those who allowed me to quote them and tell stories from their lives, my undying gratitude for your trust in how those quotes and stories might turn out: Jan Bothwell, Paul Bothwell, Brenda Bradley, Ginger Brasher-Cunningham, Milton Brasher-Cunningham, Elizabeth Cernoia, Pete Cernoia, Kay Price Brinkley, Clint Hinote, Myra Rubiera Hinote, Julie Miller Huffaker, Vince Huffaker, Beth Jackson-Jordan, David Jordan, Virginia Kearney, Kelly Monroe Kullberg, Julia Lisella, Steve Moore, Julie Pennington-Russell, Mark Pomilio, Shannon Roberts, Jason Rogers, Mary Anne Severino, Frank Shushok, Christy Somerville, Man-Wah Tan, Ching-Hua Tseng, and Lu Treadwell, Cathy Trotter Wilson, Kevin Wilson and my small group at Calvary Baptist, who walked with us and prayed with us through our adoption process.

Quite a few friends deserve extra recognition—your names are among those above—for not simply asking but showing up to whisk away my kids to play when I needed more time to think. For several of you, it was your ferocious prayers and spunk and humor that became invaluable during this season of life—and still is. Some of you—and you know who you are—keep my kids in essential Boston Red Sox attire and cool wardrobes and not-sensible shoes, and I thank you.

As one of the deadlines approached on this book, my mother called to ask if she could come visit—and proceeded to read bedtime stories and cook and even paint a kitchen at my house, with abandon—allowing me to keep my nose to the grindstone and keyboard. And my father, who misses her painfully when she's gone, added his help by supporting her fully in coming.

My thanks to professor and speaker Tony Campolo, who, when I was once in the depths of despair over whether a writer could do anything worthwhile and directly beneficial for people living in poverty, offered a simple, matter-of-fact *well, of course*. And to Nobel laureate Betty Williams, who was generous in telling my husband and me stories of her life and her work as we drove the two-hour trip to the Dallas airport, and who was a key person in inspiring this book. And to Ralph Wood, to whose scholarship I turned when I needed confirmation of a Flannery O'Connor story. And to Benita Walker, an amazing woman of faith— and connections.

I'm grateful as well to the management and staff of Chick-fil-A in Brentwood, Tennessee, who not only tolerated my early morning presence, but graciously even pretended that tapping away on a laptop there in a vinyl booth was almost normal.

My warm thanks to my nonfiction agent Katie Boyle of Veritas Literary Agency, who makes contract negotiation an actually pleasant process.

To a person, the editorial, marketing, art, and production teams of Water-Brook/Random House have been affirming, encouraging, smart, and a genuine pleasure to deal with at every stage. I've felt privileged to work with you.

My "forever and always" love to my daily inspirations and the treasures of my life, Julia, Justin, and Jasmine. Our little Jasmine, whose addition to our family occurred during the writing of this book, was a gift of grace and the best lesson of all. And just now, even as I type her name and this sentence, she is crawling into my lap to help pound the keyboard and share my iced tea—as involved with both her parents' work as ever.

And finally, a whole-heart shout of *thank you you're amazing I love you* to the biggest single contributor to this book and the most ardent supporter of my work, my husband Todd, my co-parent, fellow pilgrim, and best friend, who makes every day an adventure and a delight.

Mistakes Under Sail

The fact that my husband, Todd, and I ever ended up married with children began, to be frank, with a mistake. A whole series of them. The one that started it all took place on a sailboat with one too many sails—and it only had two.

But I'm getting ahead of myself…

In every home we've owned, I've proudly displayed the framed print Todd gave me as a wedding gift. It's an attractive New England scene, a watercolor of white sailboats skimming across the Charles River Basin. The river, colored a little bluer than life, separates the funky, hemp-twisted Cambridge from tweedy, cobble-stoned Boston.

For us, the picture is far more important than a pretty painting of a place where we dated and later lived in a newlywed nest—a beloved rent-controlled apartment with a bathroom down a public hall and Italian landlords who made apricot wine and banged on the pipes when we waltzed too wildly on the wood floors over their heads.

Dinner guests—the polite ones at least—comment on the watercolor print regularly. Then, if they want to eat the cheesecake perched on the sideboard, they have to appear to want to hear our story.

There are two versions of the story: the short one, in which Todd and I gaze into each other's eyes and recall how that's where he popped the question, and the longer, unpasteurized version in which we gaze into each other's eyes and recall that that's where we nearly ended our love and our lives.

Both versions are true. The second is the more ugly and interesting story. And okay, maybe a little more true than the first.

Sometimes we merely exchange a bemused glance with each other, a look that says we're both a little startled to see our partner standing there after all this time—I distinctly remember one of us saying nearly two decades ago that we should be "just good friends."

And then we refill the iced tea.

But for the guests who want to hear more, or at least want to get on with the cheesecake, we explain.

Romance on the High Seas

This is an instance when a picture is *not* worth a thousand words—we writers cling to these moments.

That particular watercolor print of white sails and blue skies suggests harmony, calm, and quiet romance.

This wasn't the case.

Todd knew I'd been the Head Sailing Instructor—still the best job title I've ever had—at a swanky, Very Cool Camp for boys in the Blue Ridge Mountains. Paradise was what it was: a college woman in charge of a fleet of sailboats and half-day lessons on Lake Eden (really, that was its name) encircled by mountains and male, college-aged staffers—all those Adams for just a handful of us Eves. I've no idea why they paid me.

But Todd, my boyfriend of only a year, was still short on details of my past—as some boyfriends ought to be kept. What he didn't know was this: I'd been hired by the Very Cool Camp to teach horseback riding, a skill I knew at least enough about to assist a pro. I grew up in the hills of East Tennessee, and a hankering for horses comes as natural to me as my aversion to shoes. But at the last minute, the camp had been blessed by a string of well-trained horses from Hollins College that came equipped with their own string of instructors. So the Very Cool Camp put me in charge of sailing, which was fine with me since the dock had fewer flies and the new title—Head Sailing Instructor—had a nice ring to it.

Except that I'd been sailing only once in my life.

So out I went my first day of work to master a sport in a day. How hard could it be?

A storm was brewing on Lake Eden that afternoon, and the mountains kept the winds circling in a bowl. And I sat on that Mixmaster of a lake and capsized my boat so many times I lost count—easily in the double digits. A crowd of counselors and camp secretaries and random Appalachian Trail hikers and Pisgah National Forest rangers started to form.

Fortunately, in the one prior day in my life that I'd sailed, I'd learned how to right a capsized boat: information I now needed. So I righted the boat. And righted the boat. And righted the boat, until only my Timex was still ticking. The rest of me—including my favorite Georgia Tech T-shirt and my carefully-curled-that-morning hair—was swamped out and washed up.

"Who the fried okra is *that*?" I was told the waterfront director wanted to know.

"That," the cook told him, "is your new Head Sailing Instructor."

As I disappeared under the water again.

But I came up with a couple of ideas by late afternoon. One was to read the Boy Scout sailing merit-badge book I'd been given. The other was to have my campers introduce themselves on the first day of class and give information about any sailing experience they might have.

Now, a certain class of people sends their kids to this Very Cool Camp, and I knew there would always be a Willoughby Alston Winston III, who'd raced Laser sailboats with his daddy that spring in Bermuda, and a Drayton Sheffield Medfield Jr., who'd just been given his own Hobie Cat for making his bed three days in a row. I loved these boys, sometimes because they were charming and well mannered, but always because they made me look almost competent. I could let them have the thrill of demonstrating for the class, say, a broad reach, while I explained what it was. If I earned a reputation as a teacher who emphasized class participation, it was because I had no clue what I was doing.

So I learned from the Boy Scouts and from the blond surfer dude who was, unaccountably, a riflery instructor that year, and from my Richie Rich boys who thought I was sweet to let them show off what they knew. When I wasn't lifeguarding during free swim—I did have a little training for that—I snuck out a boat and practiced.

So Todd, knowing only my former job title, had convinced the good people at Community Sailing in Boston that they should be eager to ignore their own strict regulations. Despite their number one rule that no one could rent a boat without first taking a series of lessons, he assured them that I—whom they'd never met—was a clear exception because (a) I was an accomplished sailor, needing not one word of advice, and (b) the good people of Community Sailing would be forever remembered as accomplices in the greatest love story of the century. He warned them, too, that I was a shy person, and modest, one of those self-effacing southern types—they'd seen *The Andy Griffith Show*, right? I would claim to know little of sailing, even though I had been, as they would see for themselves, a Head Sailing Instructor.

Now the sailboats at the Very Cool Camp were Sunfish, little one-mast dinghies with only a mainsail and a single halyard to hoist it and only a mainsheet and rudder to guide it. The Lasers at Boston Community Sailing boasted masts that reached like Jack's beanstalk up into the clouds. The higher the mast, I recalled, the bigger the sail, and the bigger the sail, the faster the boat. I could see all the way up to the clouds that I was in trouble.

I turned to the Community Sailing staff. "Y'all are nice to give me a chance, but I don't really think I'm expert enough to sail these kinds of boats."

They exchanged glances that said, *He predicted she'd say this* and *You know how those southerners are* and *Get a load of that accent.* They pointed to a slip. "Number 58 will be yours."

"But," I tried again, "see, I don't know how to work a jib. Or—"

"You were a Head Sailing Instructor," they said. "You'll be fine." And they untied boat 58 from the dock.

And that's how we came to be in the Charles River Basin on a Laser careening toward the Longfellow Bridge. Unprepared for the boat's speed, and its quicksilver response to every twitch of the tiller, I wrenched the rudder side to side, overcompensating each time, misjudging, sending the bow plunging right to left, the boat heeling hard on its side, the mainsail full and flying across with each tack.

It was clear to me where this would end: our splayed arms and legs permanently pasted to the pilings of the Longfellow Bridge like a Road Runner cartoon, our final words blaming each other.

After lurching at the last minute away from the bridge, we narrowly missed ramming into several dozen innocent vessels, and we spent the rest of the afternoon ducking the boom as it swung for our heads. Except for one brief interlude when Todd, thrown across the hull but still controlling the mainsheet as I hauled on the tiller, reached into the picnic basket for something he clutched in his left hand.

"You'll have to trim the sail more," I shouted over the wind. "No, still more!"

"What about that sail up front?"

"How should I know?"

"I thought you were the Head S—"

"It's called a jib. *That's all I know, okay?*"

"But you—"

"I tried to tell you that. Back there on the dock."

He trimmed the sails, pulling the mainsheet in and the mainsail taut. The boat heeled harder to the side and we both hiked out, throwing our upper bodies out over the water for balance.

"Todd, not that much!"

"Whoa, these things can fly, huh? I had no idea!"

"Watch out for the—!"

"I thought *you* were steering!"

We swerved through a maze of suddenly very awake fellow sailors.

"Hey," Todd shouted to me, "when's the part where we slow down? When do we stop and chat?"

A rest? A chat? Couldn't he see I had my hands full keeping us from killing ourselves?

The bow plowed to the right, and as we ducked from the boom, I barked back, "This is why we call sailing a *sport*!"

I'm not clear on why he still held out the blue velvet box. And I'm not clear on what I said after I saw sparkle that wasn't water. But I don't remember a chat.

I vaguely recall my jaw dropping wide like a bigmouth bass and trying to take in what this meant. I remember there was a question, but I can't recall any answer, just both of us laughing and lurching, shouting orders to each other and ducking the boom, barely threading through boats without sending ourselves or the diamond ring down to the basin bottom.

Peering through binoculars from the watchtower, Community Sailing staff members apparently had been waiting quite some time for a two thumbs-up from Todd. When it came, we heard over the public address system, "She said *yes!* Ladies and gentlemen, there's been a proposal of marriage in boat 58, which from now on we're calling the Love Boat, and she said *yes!*"

They needed that outcome, of course, to justify having broken the rules. I remember being struck by their excitement, at other people besides the two of us having some sort of stake in how things turned out between us—and it wouldn't be the last time.

Did I say yes? Maybe I did.

At the time, though, my mind was occupied elsewhere. At the Very Cool Camp, I'd taught a class on Not Ramming the Dock, but here at Community Sailing, with the cheers still going up over the PA system, the dock seemed to be approaching way too fast. I had a huge sail, a co-captain who seemed to be taking his time loosing the halyard, and a whole lot more speed than appropriate when we started dropping the sails.

Community Sailing staff members dove headlong to catch us as we slammed into the slip. Thanks only to several sets of long, strong arms, we did not slice the keel of the Love Boat in half that day—which perhaps wouldn't have been the best way to begin our new life together: the two, committing themselves to becoming one flesh, already blasted back into two.

Lessons Learned Under Sail

The other night Todd and I passed the framed print on our way to bed. Having stayed up laughing too late again, we'd dragged ourselves, hand in hand, up the stairs. He stopped and cocked his head at the print and said, "You know, if we'd only known then how symbolic that day was for our marriage."

I knew exactly what he meant—and it wasn't a sweet nothing meant to sweep me off my slippered feet, past flossing and straight into bed. He intended to jab at us both, referring to a death-defying beginning that fittingly preceded what was to come: The thrills. The spills. Mr. Toad's Wild Ride on water.

In fact, we learned a lot about parenting and professional life from sailing. For instance:

1. Pay attention to atmospheric conditions.
2. If you can't be skilled, be persistent.
3. If you sail with a crew, you must work as a team and must understand—and respect—what the others can and can't do.
4. Ignore most spectators' reactions, especially the stares and guffaws.
5. Seek out wise, seasoned sailors. Ask questions, watch closely, and be ready to learn.
6. Without at least some kind of wind, the boat doesn't move forward. Complete calm, therefore, would not be your primary goal.
7. No sailors are as good as they can be until they've weathered a lot of rough weather.

The whole thing, of course, was Todd's fault. And you can tell him I said so. Not only the sailing that day, but also the fact that we ended up married—married with jobs we love and kids we adore and lives together lived out with a big wind at our backs and full sails and not always much in the way of brakes.

Which brings us back to mistakes and how sometimes two professional callings and a marriage that turned into a family—which is also a calling—can have their roots in the "how did this happen?" It happened because of lots of mistakes and one boat with a very tall mast. But for all its lurching and heeling and ducking the boom, for all its past storms and rare moments of quiet, this marriage has become a place of comfort and purpose and peace. And passion. Did I mention passion? Most certainly passion.

Who would have thought?

Not always smooth sailing. But what fun would that be, anyway?

Sailing and the Three-Career Marriage

Two High-Energy Sports

I should begin by saying that those gentle readers looking for a how-to book in which the author conducts a step-by-step, see-how-I-did-it, seven-day process of personal enlightenment, marital tranquility, parental omniscience, stock-market savvy, and washboard abdominal muscles should look elsewhere—and quickly. My résumé is a long list of high-energy and low-pay positions: writer, minister, director of a food pantry for homeless families, English professor. Clearly, I never received career counseling from anyone who'd ever balanced a checkbook. My eating habits feature regular clandestine meetings with artificially flavored chocolate minidoughnuts. And my spiritual journey includes plenty of not-suitable-for-framing moments. But I'm crazy about my family, and I'm crazy about my work both inside and outside the home.

I'm what our culture calls a "working mom," although I'd also be the first to protest that this is a brutally unjust designation—suggesting the "stay-at-home" or "nonworking" mom is wolfing bonbons from a vinyl recliner where she's watching soap operas.

Of course, writing doesn't look like a "real" job anyway. My neighbor-friend back in rural North Carolina used to take great delight in reporting to my husband that he'd spotted me once again out in the gazebo with a glass of iced tea. The fact that I was working, laptop on lap, just as he was working out of his testosterone-leaking, blue pickup deterred him not in the least. But when I don my college professor's hat, I join the suited work force and, therefore, the coffeepot conversations: comparing day cares and potty-training methods and teenage dating dramas and stacks of ungraded research papers shrieking for subject-verb agreement.

So as a vocationally ambiguous "both and neither" in the polarized worlds of working and stay-at-home mothers, I've shared in the cresting waves and undertows of emotion from both sides of the International Maternal Divide: The whispered feelings of loss or the guilty admissions of dearly bought freedom. The wistful sighs. The bristlings at stereotypes. The pangs I feel on the days I'm the one in the power suit and hear the happy squeal of "Mommy!" from the other side of the restaurant as I wonder what my own child is doing just then. The frustration—even anger—when I'm the one in the sweats, holding tiny hands coated in jam, and I pass the group in pumps and pressed linen. I want to stop them and explain, "See, I know, like you do, what it's like to have my opinions valued by people in power—it's just that these days those people all happen to be under three feet tall."

Women are capable of so much good but also so much damage toward ourselves and one another—subtly lobbing grenades of guilt or condescension across the battleground of work and home, and then, back in the trenches, turning our biggest guns on our own heads. And meanwhile the men struggle to march out as fully engaged fathers and fully supportive husbands and fully proficient professionals—a complex, multipart role they may never have seen modeled.

Here's one thing I've learned by illicit listening: among those of us lucky enough to get to make choices about whether we marry and if we have children and what we pursue as a profession, there may be a few full-time, outside-the-home moms who have never missed a moment's sleep panicking over the baby's adjustment to day care. There may also be a few full-time, at-home moms who've quit meaningful jobs for the sake of kids and never once missed getting to engage a part of the brain that does not store the names and corresponding colors of the Teletubbies. But most of us live somewhere in the glorious, anxious center. We feel torn some days and nuts some days, and every day, at least when we remember, we feel privileged—rich in the simple, spectacular gift of loving and being loved and trying to live a life of purpose. At least that's the goal, is it not?

I wrote this book not because I have The Answers, which I now dispense on index cards from my children's lemonade stand and my home-office desk, but because I have very real questions about this very real thing so many of us are trying to do: treating our child-rearing, our profession (whether full time, part time, or on hold), and our spouse's profession (whether full time, part time, or on hold) as three separate callings that must function *together,* with respect and care and celebration for each other. My friends Ray and Gloria White Hammond term this the "three-career marriage."

I wrote this book because I'm an impatient, notoriously time-challenged person who struggles for work that is important and a marriage that is vibrant and a spirit that is at least sometimes focused outside my own fantastically selfish concerns. I also struggle for happy, generous, well-adjusted children and a blue jeans size vaguely reminiscent of what it was *before* those happy, generous, well-adjusted children. At times I'm in touch with reality enough to know that I don't excel at all of these things every day. So I'm not the model or the guru. But I do listen to the lives around me. And here and there, I've learned from my mistakes.

My own three-career marriage has seen its share of storms—hurricane seasons, in fact—and I owe its survival to the tender mercies of a God who has taught me about the firestorming power of forgiveness, both given and received. I owe its survival, too, to a husband who has been my fellow traveler and fellow seeker and toughest combatant and dearest, best friend. And I owe it to Gloria and Ray, both medical doctors, both African Methodist Episcopal ministers and civic leaders in Boston, both devoted parents, who were brave and real and loving enough to speak openly about their own storms. Just knowing they'd survived—and now thrived—helped us get through our tumultuous years. Back then, in the midst of the worst of the squalls, I remember thinking that if we made it through, maybe someday some kind of wisdom learned in my own ugly storms would help pull someone else out of the sea.

Wrestling the Questions

How *do* we stay invested in our own professional callings when our children—from the moment we first feel them stir inside us or fix our eyes on their gorgeous, wondering faces in the orphanage—have held our hearts and our Day-Timers in their gummy-beared hands? How do we give them the emotional, spiritual, and physical nurturing they deserve from us and still perform in the workplace so that we not only pay our bills but do work that answers a different calling, that stretches our talents, and that taps into at least one day of one class of all that formal education?

When do the demands—and delights—of infants or toddlers or teenagers insist that someone set down the briefcase or the toolbox or the judge's gavel for a while and take time off from work outside the home? And is there a way to put a professional life on hold and still be respected when it's time to come roaring back from the nursery?

How do we cheerlead for our spouse's work to the point of being willing to uproot our own job, find a new pediatrician, repot the petunias, and rebury the dog's bones in a foreign backyard? And when do we expect our spouses and kids and dogs to do the same for us—for that position we've prepared all our lives for, that chance to play in the big leagues? How do we answer a calling to our vocation as *parents* as well as doctors and teachers and musicians and scientists and writers and social workers?

As I've wrestled with these questions, I've needed more than a little help from my friends, near and far-flung, who have shared their stories over tamales and Pad Thai and sweet cheese croissants, by the Play-Doh shelf of the preschool and the photocopy machine in the faculty office. Much of their wisdom is included here.

To broaden the scope, I've also talked with individuals and couples who aren't personal friends. Some of them are famous and fairly inaccessible, actually, and their assistant's secretary's personal trainer's dog groomer had to screen my criminal record and kindergarten transcript before graciously granting a meeting. But they love what they do as parents and professionals, and they know the struggles to get to that place. So it's worth noting what they've done well and where they've crashed—before they then continued the ride. It is, after all, not some final destination but the journey itself that we're called to. This is what the beginners among us, like me, are slowly learning.

Tired of the Circus Act

Juggling or balancing acts are two metaphors we often use to describe professional couples with children or aging parents or other in-your-face (or in-your-lap) family concerns. But that makes us all circus performers: Clowns to be laughed at, falling out of the tiny car in our too-big shoes. Or trapeze artists to be gasped over, our partners grabbing our ankles as we free-fall toward the floor. Either way, it's not much of an image for a family life or a career.

Of course managing career and family is a juggling act. Of course we need balance and coordination. But I'd rather not be a circus performer.

Combining family life with one's own work and one's spouse's work—whether or not both of those are always outside the home—is more about seasons than performance. It's about mapping out those seasons as they come. There are evenings for teaching a teenager to drive, midnights for steaming a shower for the toddler with croup, and wee morning hours for meeting a publisher's deadline. Life ought to expand and shift and attend to all these things—though, ideally, not all in the same night.

Combining family and professional life is about treating three callings as always connected, never allowing one part to shift without understanding how that will swing the whole ship. It's about realizing that if the compass only points to one spouse's professional talents and dreams, then the other spouse's gifts and the children's welfare will get lost at sea. It's important to put a few expectations in the plan—*till death do us part,* for example—but the more we remain open to change, the better the possibility of making the whole thing function together.

So you can see how the sailboat that began my own marriage-turned-family-plus-two-careers became an image for me of what we are trying to do.

Done poorly, we drown.

Or the crew mutinies.

Or we end up marooned and blaming it all on the crew of buffoons—which is funny only in old sitcom reruns.

Done well, sailing's the best sport in the world. Some days it's exhausting. Some days the seas swell and swirl and the sky loses its blue. And yet...

And yet the sails fill. The sailors might need to hike over the water for balance, legs and sails and ropes all pulling together. But they are holding strong. Holding on. And loving the strength of the wind.

Against Wind and Tide

Changing the World, the Diapers,
and the Printer Cartridge

S everal years ago, I was droning through directions for a writing exercise in a freshman composition class. It was at a top-tier university in the Northeast, and the students had long since mastered the art of appearing riveted by their instructor's every golden word. They were sitting forward in their seats, their wide, I-love-your-class-Professor eyes fixed on mine. But I know a vacant stare when I see one; I'd just slid into a good one myself.

So in a burst of creativity and survival, I switched tacks, taking the emphasis off Your Friend the Semicolon and focusing instead on how they could make the *substance* of their writing compelling. I had them compose a third-person interview with themselves as they hoped to be when they were thirty.

"Dream big," I told them.

I was fast approaching thirty myself at the time and was painfully aware of all the things still left undone—including adding the pitter-patter of little feet in my home. It was beginning to occur to me that this should perhaps move up in its ranking on the to-do list.

My students' interviews with their thirty-year-old selves didn't surprise me in their cleverness or their vaulting ambition—they weren't paying that kind of tuition to prepare themselves for delivering newspapers door to door, honorable as that might be. I expected, and got, a couple of dentists and neurosurgeons, a CEO, a Supreme Court judge, a boatload of attorneys, a cardiologist, radiologist, anthropologist, and journalist, the latter two whose beachfront lifestyles were to be funded, I assume, by the timely demise of a wealthy aunt.

But here's what I didn't expect: the stark contrast between how the women and the men addressed the subject of children. Most of the male students awarded themselves multiple offspring by age thirty. They also envisioned their wives as the soon-to-be-highly-educated women who were sharing the classroom with them: the budding neurosurgeons and judges.

"Okay," I said after they read their interviews aloud to the class, "these are eloquent. Intriguing. Logically organized—mostly. We'll get to that. But could I just ask: who is with those four gorgeous little children during the day?"

Most of the men shrugged. "I dunno. Never thought about that."

The women squirmed in their seats. Their essays and their eyes showed knee-deep anxiety over how they would follow their dreams and their callings and still have the families that most of them wanted.

One of the women lashed out, "How could you guys *not* think about this?"

One of the men plunged in, "Well, I'll tell you this: no kid of mine will be farmed out to day care. All I want is to be a great dad."

"So," I asked him, "someone's staying home full time then, Darrell the Aspiring Dentist?"

"Yeah. Sure."

"Who?"

"Um…well, my wife, I guess. A dentist can't just take time off like that to stay home."

"But your wife, Sally the Surgeon, can?"

"Well…yeah. Sure. *And* she would want to."

A couple of women in the class rumbled.

"No," I turned to them, "let him talk. No one's allowed to intimidate anyone else. Only ask genuine questions." I turned back to him. "You may be right. She may very well want to. Lots of women do."

He nodded.

A couple of the women glowered at me.

One whispered, "I would want to. You know, if I could."

"And," I said, "you should be respected for that. *But* what if Darrell the Dentist's wife, Sally the Surgeon, feels she…" I was distracted by one student, Tina, who looked as if she might lunge across the classroom at Darrell. I ceded the floor.

"What if," Tina tore into him, "she *can't* take time off in her field without falling too far behind, or what if she doesn't *want* to? What if she wants to be as great a mom as you do a dad, but what if she also loves what she does for a job, and what if she's doing great stuff?"

He shrugged again. "We can do without the second income for a while."

"But what if she's not working only for the money? What if money wasn't the point; she was just doing some pretty cool stuff? You know, like discovering a cure for breast cancer?"

Seeing which way the winds of dating possibilities were blowing, most of the other men abandoned Darrell right there—so much for drum-beating, pipe-smoking male solidarity.

"*I,*" one young man purred sweetly, "would let my wife do whatever she wanted." He looked around the class for doe-eyed adulation.

"*Let* her?" the women cried.

Frightened, he looked to me for protection.

"Let me reference," I said professorially, "yesterday's lecture on the importance of *choosing just the right word for your target audience.*" I left him to twist in the wind.

"I," tried a fraternity pledge, "would *support* my wife in whatever *she* decided to do: work part time or full time or not at all. *Totally supportive.* That's me." A charming dimple dug its way into his cheek. He might need a date for the Friday-night mixer, but he was also a sweet guy and he meant what he said.

"So it's all on her, then?" Tina demanded. "You take no responsibility for making the decision?"

When I called time to turn our attention back to the way these essays were *written*—that was the task at hand, after all—the tension had nearly flattened us all. Some of the women were white-knuckled, clutching their desks with preemptive worry or rage for their futures. Some of the men sat stunned, their hopes and ideas for the future suddenly in question; most of them were strangers in a land their fathers had never entered.

I've since realized this classroom discussion captured the confusion, anxiety, and judgment that rifles through the professional/family debates—both the public squabbles and the battles stirring inside our own homes and minds.

Had I written this book before I'd had children myself, I very well might've written with the naiveté of some of the young men in my class. My experience would have lacked something—despair, for example. But it would also have lacked the more mature, hard-won hope that follows despair, the hope that reaches beyond that tension to a place of joy.

That Marvelous Mess

Let me be perfectly frank: my professional life was killed, and only later reborn, by a birth—the marvelous mess, the loud, bloody, boisterous coming of my second child, a son. And neither the birth nor the rebirth was pretty. My son, at least, did grow fine lungs and blond ringlets and cherub cheeks on what had been a decidedly Winston Churchill face. My writing life, though, sputtered and gasped and spasmed for long months. How exactly does one create characters who live and breathe and glitter and swagger when you, their creator, can hardly hold your head upright? I was exhausted down to my brainstem.

My son's three-weeks-early entrance into this world occurred soon after I ignored pleas to take it easy and instead vigorously, happily shoveled a horse stall. I would not be stopped; I would not slow down. I would be a great mom to our first child, a daughter, and to our son on the way and still write my books and teach my classes and complete my dissertation and nurture my marriage and friendships and feed our family's menagerie of abandoned animals and grow spiritually and thin up the thighs that had suddenly discovered they'd turned thirty-five along with the rest of me.

But my son upended my lists of "Urgent: To Be Done Today" and in the process toppled my sense of myself as a working writer and as a contributing member of society. I'd hardly been turning the world upside down, but I'd marched in my own barefooted way in the ranks of the well-intended. Before I'd had children and even during my daughter's toddler years, I'd run a clothes closet and food pantry serving homeless and low-income families in Cambridge, Massachusetts. As a college professor and as a minister charged with community needs, I'd ladled in soup kitchens and sweated with Habitat for Humanity and spoken to Harvard and Wellesley and MIT groups on caring deeply about the hungry worldwide and in our own back alleys.

And then in fiction and nonfiction, I'd written about what all this had taught me over the years, about the ways my heart had expanded from its tight little Christmas-tin, sheltered existence.

But no more. On a good day, I might stagger my way to mail a check for hunger relief. But on no day in those months after my second child's birth did I have enough time or functioning neurons that I could write anything outside my increasingly dull doctoral dissertation. This writing didn't count in my mind as part of my real writing life; it was only filing for my professors' union card, meeting an academic deadline that had for years been fee-fi-fo-fumming toward me like a giant who would eat me for dinner if I didn't outrun him first.

Among our colleagues in New England were Norm, a Congregational minister, and Peggy, a writer and professor. As the parents of two cherished, special-needs children, they say they discovered that raising only one child compared with multiple children was deceptively easy: just a couple with a mascot. Certainly, that was the sea change waiting for us—from mascot to barely contained madness.

My older daughter was the kind of baby who dozed, snored, and cooed coast to coast when we were once bumped from economy to first class (much to the horror of the full-fare passengers) on a trip from Boston to Los Angeles. She seemed to have found her people in first class, in fact. As the warm nuts and chilled wine passed over her snuggled head, her self-satisfied smile seemed to say, *Ah, to be where I belong at last.*

But my son—oh, my son. A gorgeous, beloved little man, he became hungry every hour on the hour; his fullback figure testified to his demanding mess-hall schedule. His inner-ear apparatus caused him no end of pain, and for a time our primary residence became the pediatrician's office. Then, too, my son simply did not require much sleep. We were building a house in Texas at the time, and Justin dozed in the lumber aisles of Home Depot—the scent of sawdust seemed to calm him—but he never ceded to the morning and afternoon two-hour-apiece monster naps our first child had given me.

Between naps and evenings and alternating work schedules, my husband and I had both managed to work full time with our first child while having her in outside child care only part of one day a week. Now, in my son's infancy, our family's having just moved, with my trusted co-parent in an unexpectedly demanding new job and all the best child-care facilities booked solid and no friends and no family and very little REM sleep, I paid dearly for the scorn I'd once harbored toward parents who claimed they could "get nothing done." What little of my dissertation got done happened at three in the morning with a nursing baby in one arm, my other arm free to attend to the chocolate minidoughnuts and the ancient, wheezing computer.

I ceased showering regularly.

The Case of the Disappearing Woman

We'd just moved a thousand miles from where I was at home personally and professionally—from where the mountains and forests and shores were for me, like Anne Shirley and her Lake of Shining Waters in *Anne of Green Gables,* "scope for the imagination." I'd left an enviable lineup of classes I'd been scheduled to teach, a tight circle of friends, and flocks of extended family within easy driving distance. When it became clear we'd be shoehorning our lives into suburban rental housing for a number of months, I surrendered a racehorse I'd adopted, Zhaozlong, who in his career made more money than I ever did—and had far better legs. Now it was just our little foursome, plus the remaining four-legged crowd, in a grim 1970s house distinguished by dark paneling, a mountain range of moving boxes identically labeled STUFF, and a floor carpeted in stained, off-white nylon plush and the illegible research notes I sifted through daily on the dining room floor.

Together, Todd and I had planned what this new season of life ought to look like for us: I would stop teaching for a while and instead hole up and finish my dissertation. He would make an impression as a hard worker at a new job. And we both assumed it would be no problem for me to continue with my professional life. As his big sister had done, Justin could sleep in the swing or sweetly stack blocks by Mommy's computer.

Our son, however, had apparently misread his explicit instructions.

My husband's new job, meanwhile, brought us in contact with a steady stream of remarkable speakers, people who'd written the books I wanted to write, who headed the international development agencies I wanted to run, who'd won the Nobel Peace Prize and rocked audiences by the thousands on issues about which I didn't even have time to read.

Others were changing the course of history, and me, I was changing diapers and sheets and sometimes, for kicks, a computer printer cartridge.

"Life has its seasons," older women consoled me. "You need to be patient."

Of course they were right. Who would trade anything for those soul-still, perfect moments of rocking your baby? Who would want to rush that?

But I knew too—and this scared me—that this was a crazed, not even rational attachment I had to these children, and that it wasn't going away. I would never again become *less* concerned with investing time in my family just because someday my children would be in school. These relationships had me bound at the heart, and I sensed the rest of my professional life would be, by my choice, at their mercy.

That might have been okay had my passion for my writing life and all those change-the-world instincts backed off and made room for the newly enlarged, so-happy-I-can't-see-straight loves of my personal life. But instead I began to feel pulled like taffy, kneaded and stretched and sliced into pieces.

And invisible. Some days I was sure I'd disappeared, nothing remaining of me but a blue nursing blouse with baby spit-up on the shoulder. I knew for certain my brain had already rotted right there in my head—my head that had disappeared.

"Why?" I demanded of my husband as he came home from work and I sat on the floor surrounded by mounds of stackable Little Tikes toys, as well as the two tykes themselves. My dissertation research notes, untouched that whole day, were ditched three rooms and a lifetime away. "Why do we bother to teach women to read?"

Even as I grew into myself more fully as a mother and fell daily more in love with my kids, I felt I'd abandoned a crucial part of what God made me to be. In the midst of Cheerios dust and diaper wipes, I wondered if I would ever see that professional woman again.

Learning from Dead Dissertation Research

Then, during Justin's first couple of years, two things happened to backflip my perspective and plunk me down hard. And a book that had been conceived with my son—though I didn't know it then—began to take shape.

First came the tragedies—not always my own but still personal and all around me. My husband's work for a large private university in central Texas positioned him as the first to receive news of a crisis: the SUV rollover, the sudden collapse of a nineteen-year-old jogger, the frat-party stunt, the innocent flip off a porch that ended in paralysis, the Yield sign that failed to catch a young driver's eye, the heart failure of an expectant mother…

"It must be so hard to live in your house," people said.

Hard, yes. We cried a lot there. Prayed a lot, too. I heard the phone ring at wee hours, and my heart seized up. Through the everlasting "what now?" I waited for the name, not knowing if this time it would be a personal friend, a part of the family, a faculty member we'd just seen at dinner, or a student who'd just been in our home.

Hard, yes. But in our house you didn't forget that life is a gift, and you unwrap it each day with care. You didn't forget that education and work, particularly work that one *wants* to do, are privileges to be viewed with a caught-breath kind of awe. You didn't forget that if you get to make choices about a career path, if you get to make real decisions about where you'll live, if you get to think through how to channel your skills, if you get to tuck fully fed kids into bed, then you're one of the very fortunate and very few in our world.

The second thing that helped pull me out of my hole was, ironically, one of the things that had landed me there in the first place: my research.

During all those many midnights at my computer as I tried to tap life into dead dissertation research, I was struck with the gumption, the vision, the raw political power that one unlikely figure possessed. I began to feel like I knew her— and her life made my life look calm.

A small-statured woman who wrote stories to help pay family bills, she was the mother of six and living in a small town in mid-nineteenth-century Maine. Her husband, Calvin, a dedicated but financially struggling professor, saw genius in his wife's writing, despite the fact that her books had so far sold only as sentimental romances.

"My dear, you must be a literary woman. It is so written in the book of fate.... Make all your calculations accordingly,"[1] he told her. So mid-nineteenth-century Calvin learned more of housecleaning and child-rearing and made himself into an early *Working Families* kind of guy.

One day when Calvin was out of town on business, the youngest of the children became gravely ill. The infant died in his mother's arms. She wrote to her husband that she couldn't bear up under the pain; only one thing sustained her: she was praying that somehow, some way, God might bring some kind of good out of the grief that had swallowed her whole.

She wept for her own loss, for the child that disease had wrenched from her. Then she agonized in a way she never had before—for slave mothers whose children were being wrenched from them on the auction block. So she wept for those mothers, too, and vowed to do what she could to fight so brutal a system.

Though she'd long considered writing to be her sacred profession, her "paper pulpit," Harriet Beecher Stowe struggled to balance that drive with those unending domestic duties. Finding time in her life to write was always, she said, "rowing against wind and tide."[2] But out of her own still-bleeding grief and her newly heightened sensitivity to slave mothers' tears, she sat down at her kitchen table each day and, surrounded by the thunder of little feet, penned the novel *Uncle Tom's Cabin*.

By far the bestselling book of the nineteenth century, *Uncle Tom's Cabin* became the turning point in the beginning of the end of slavery. Whatever the controversies surrounding it today—its disturbing racial stereotypes, for example—the novel achieved more than all the other antislavery propaganda combined and forever altered the course of American history.

As an economically powerless woman in the 1850s, a too-busy mother of six, Harriet had every reason to stand by, like most citizens of her country, and watch the political wheels turn, and muse, *What could one person—especially one woman, a mother—do after all?*

But precisely because she was a woman and a mother, she couldn't stand by. And she didn't. She rowed against wind and tide. Her husband, who believed in her talent, rowed right beside her, rooting her on. And her sister, Catharine Beecher, arrived to help take care of the house and the children. And Harriet, writing on, driven by what she called a divine purpose, accepted the help of the hardworking family around her.

And the world became a far better place.

Working to Help Families Work

This set me to wondering: What could I do, crazed as I was with diapers and dissertation, to make some sort of difference? And who were the women and men out there like me—or like I wanted to be—who were "rowing against wind and tide" inside and outside their homes, who were following both personal and professional callings, who were changing the world not in spite of their children, but *because* of them?

So along with two little ones and the early prayers for the third, a new book began to take shape. Long midnights of words slowly appeared on the screen, and then came the idea that half the royalties of the book could go to women and families just beginning their own businesses in impoverished countries: microdevelopment loans. The words flowed then, in torrents. What if, in the midst of my own working family, I could write about the privilege of personal and professional calling?

Unlike Harriet Beecher Stowe, I didn't see before me one specific social institution I hoped to attack and bring down—except, perhaps, poverty, such a manyheaded monster that it seems naive to give it only one name. But like Harriet, I had a professional life that pounded its fists to live even in the midst of the smothering demands of my personal life. And also like her, my personal life, especially my children, had made me feel in a new and more urgent way the anguish of parents who had little choice in how they could feed or care for their children. Suddenly, something as simple as giving my baby Tylenol to bring down a raging fever and holding him as his body cooled would bring me to tears for the mothers whose babies burned on in their arms.

And like Harriet, too, I'd found an extraordinary life partner who believed in the idea of God-given gifts and that a family's calculations, complex as they might

be, ought to work not only toward the health of the marriage and the best interest of children, but also toward those gifts getting used.

And I lived the book as I wrote it.

Blue Basket and Beltway

I was endlessly curious about how the speakers who passed through the university
in our town managed their lives: *Why do you feel drawn to this work? What in your
personal life influenced that? How have you approached the demands of your family
and work? Besides the obvious tensions and pulls on your time, are there ways in which
your personal and professional lives actually enrich each another?*

Since a stranger's pummeling another human being with personal questions is
considered odd, and maybe a little psychotic, I decided to make interviews a part
of my book: socially sanctioned nosiness.

So I begged, borrowed, and wheedled my way into interview after interview,
some by phone or e-mail and some in person. At one point I was trying to secure
a conversation with a Prominent Member of the United States President's cabinet.
I'd chatted my way up the ranks from the maid of the hairdresser of the assistant's
assistant, as I recall. I had one final clearance interview with the Prominent Assistant just under the Prominent Person. My husband remapped his day to cover our
daughter's pickup from school, but I assured him I didn't need him to cover anything more. No, I had it *all under control.*

I put our son, by now a toddler, down for a long winter's nap. I watched him
close his sweet, baby blue eyes, heard his breathing become steady and even.

I crept downstairs to the phone. Just in time: Washington called.

Nervously pacing the floor as I spoke, I was midstream in describing the serious, substantive nature of the book. The Prominent Assistant seemed almost convinced but not quite. I lowered my voice to sound still more serious, still more
convincing.

It was at this point that my safely napping son appeared at the door, beaming.
He kangarooed circles around me. Then he snatched something from the kitchen
counter and placed it on his head.

"Look at me, Mommy!" he squealed.

I ignored him, of course.

I covered my outside ear to hear the important words of the Prominent Assistant.

"Look at me, Mommy!" Justin shouted, bouncing up almost to my chest.

I smiled sweetly at him, yanked his favorite puzzles from the shelf onto the floor, then ducked away, cupping the phone as I spoke to Washington of possible publishers.

"*Mommy!*"

I held my finger over my lips and scowled my worst scowl and tried, at the assistant's request, to read a few sample interview questions.

My son only bounced higher, which gave his lungs still more air.

"*Mommy, look! I have a blue basket on my head!*"

And he did. A blue woven basket that hung low on his face, his blond ringlets corkscrewing down at the sides, with a handle that looped under his chin: a football helmet in wicker.

He peered up at me from beneath the wicker and curls. "THERE'S A BLUE BASKET ON MY HEAD, MOMMY!" he bellowed. In case I hadn't noticed.

My interview chances were shot, I knew. How unprofessional could anyone be?

There was a long pause on the Washington end of the phone.

"My son," I said at last, meekly, "as you can hear, is wearing a blue basket on his head today." I didn't try to explain.

Another long pause.

"Well," said the Prominent Assistant of the Prominent Person, "that makes more sense than most of what goes on here inside the Beltway."

I chuckled politely and waited for her to permanently dismiss me. And my son. And his headgear.

"Hmm," she said. "Maybe I could borrow the basket sometime."

And she granted the interview—which I scheduled for a time when my husband would be in charge of *all* offspring.

Big People Learning to Share

And so I discovered, to my own jaw-dropping surprise, that one of the Big People in our house had not been sharing or playing well with others—and that would be me. Somehow, with the arrival of our second child and the ensuing chaos of a thousand-mile move and the shifting of professional roles, I'd slid into a kind of John Wayne approach to family and work. I swaggered through my days, at least mentally, prepared to handle all comers efficiently, quickly, and by myself. Then I wanted to gun down anyone who impeded my progress—and it was always, *always* impeded. In fact, *that*, I believe, is a toddler's entire job description.

With effort, I learned to say yes to my husband when he offered to work from home on a day when a child was home sick from school. I learned to let him make trips to the pediatrician's, where I'd somehow thought only I had the chromosomal makeup to hold out my hand for amoxicillin prescriptions. I learned he could even successfully purchase kids' shoes—though with their clothing, I still retain sole despotic power.

On the days when there seemed no way for two parents to make it all fit, I learned to say yes to the friend who insisted on picking up my kids to play, so I could work longer—and I knew she trusted me to do the same for her weeks later. I learned that hiring a baby-sitter didn't have to be a concession to weakness. My kids enjoyed the sitters—in moderation—and picked up better batting skills and piano-playing hand positions from them.

And here's what else I'm learning as a working woman and a mom and a wife: If you operate with the assumption you're in complete control of your work and your time, understand it's a delusion, and get over it. Practice saying the words "our" and "we" frequently. Remind yourself often that life and kids and work are all gifts, not to be taken for granted for even so much as a slice of a day.

I'm learning that running your fingers through your child's hair can be as soul stirring as Nobel Peace Prize laureates' speeches—and that plenty of Nobel laureates have been inspired by the same thing. And that it might be your life-upside-down kind of love for your own children that drives *why* you work, beyond just paying the bills.

I'm learning that kids, with their Vesuvius spit-ups and diaper blowouts and late-night heart-to-heart talks, will be the greatest thieves of your professional time, and for some seasons of life, that's okay—even good, when slowing down has a purpose. But kids will also help you keep focused on the point of your work in the first place. And your work just might also help guide and direct your children about where to invest their own time, their own lives.

I'm learning that the question of the Mommy Wars[3]—"working" and "non-working" moms in perpetual conflict—is the wrong question and that war is the wrong image.

I'm learning that the bewilderment and anxiety and judgment of that Freshman Comp classroom a world ago doesn't need to be the land where we set up camp.

I'm learning that weariness is sometimes just another sign that you're loved, that you love, and that you get to do what you love. There aren't many of us in this world so incredibly lucky.

I'm learning that you've got to change the world whenever you can, change the diaper whenever it's full, and change the printer cartridge whenever it isn't.

So buy yourself a blue basket to wear on your head—it helps keep perspective.

Or, here, borrow mine.

ℒaunching ℴut

Finding a Sense of Calling and Purpose

Several of the women and men I interviewed for this book defined *calling* by quoting one of my own favorite writers, Frederick Buechner. After pointing out that our word *vocation* comes from the Latin root *vocare,* "to call," Buechner suggests that "the place God calls you to is the place where your deep gladness and the world's deep hunger meet."[1]

A quick list of the professional passions of my interviewees—acting, teaching, studying law, drilling teeth—shows, from person to person, just how differently calling might look when lived out. How odd another's professional passion might look to us! Drilling teeth, for instance? *Please.* But then I see a friend shudder when she thinks of spending her mornings like me, sequestered in a room with only a laptop and a bunch of jumbled almost-ideas in her head, and I'm reminded: my idea of "deep gladness" might look more than a little loony to her, and hers might look like cruel and unusual torture to me.

Which is part of the beauty, and the mystery, of calling: it takes different shapes, life to life.

"Why," I always want to ask anyone who seems particularly engaged by their work, "do you do what you do?"

It's a fair enough question—and a good place to begin exploring the idea of calling.

Why We Do What We Do

The great southern writer Flannery O'Connor offers a wonderful answer to why we do what we do—at least one answer among many.

The already-famous author was speaking to a group of southern women about her work. I've always pictured the gathering like this: a ladies' tea, the women white-gloved and dressed in pastel florals. They are serving finger sandwiches, pimento cheese, with sweet tea. Flannery responds politely to the women who float by her and gush over her stories. Some of them seem disturbed by her fiction, concerned over how her stories depict the South. But this does not seem to perturb Flannery. "Yes," she says flatly, "yes, I meant it to be disturbing." She reads from her work, the ladies patting their gloved hands together when she is through. And then it is time for questions.

"Miss O'Connor," one woman asks, "I wonder…could you tell us why you write?"

Flannery stands there, gazing at the speaker, whose gloved hands clasp and reclasp each other as she worries that Miss O'Connor has not heard the question.

But Flannery has indeed heard the question: she has simply not understood it. When she speaks at last, her voice betrays her puzzlement. "I write," she tells the white gloves, "because I'm good at it."[2]

Because I'm good at it. Now there's a sentence a lot of us find hard to form. But it's a crucial one to consider. All kicking-the-dirt, aw-gosh humility aside, what exactly are *you* good at?

I've recently come to an insight as to why some of my women friends in traditionally male-dominated professions seemed to thrive while others were crushed: the ones who survived, even flourished, had a deep and abiding sense of the *I'm good at it*. Now, we can pretty that up and spiritualize it all we want: *God has gifted me, I'm passionate about my work…* But the essence of using, not burying, one's gifts results in a certain bowed-but-unbroken sense of being valued by God and *being good at doing this thing that you love,* however that might change season by season.

Award-winning novelist Doris Betts told me she often uses Flannery's snappy response in speeches herself. She added that it's not so arrogant as it might seem:

"It's simply her way of restating the same message as in the parable of the talents in Matthew[3]—to use whatever gift you were given is a responsibility."

Betts went on to tell me,

> I've been fortunate to work at what I've loved.... So when I read "blessed is he who has found his work,"[4] I didn't mind substituting a feminine pronoun and nodding.... To this day, very little is as satisfying to me as seeing a sentence squirm and wriggle and then click into place.

That's another good snapshot of *calling*: work that we find so deeply satisfying that we're startled to see how the little hand on the clock has spun halfway around on its face while we've been toiling away. And we're thunderstruck to discover that not everyone in the world shares our particular passion.

What *Calling* Looks Like

Bruce Kuhn is someone who cannot sit still when he speaks of his work.

My husband and I first met Bruce when he was performing a verbatim one-man act of the gospel of Luke—in King James English, of all things. A mutual friend, Kelly Monroe Kullberg, introduced us to Bruce. The previous year, while at a conference in England, Kelly had also introduced us to an extraordinarily gifted Dutch landscape painter named Hetty. I'd noticed the small prints of her seascapes before I learned their creator was there in Cambridge with us. Hetty, I recall, smiled quietly, and it struck me then she had an artist's eyes, the kind that even in the mundane moment of Nice to Meet You are soaking in a beauty most of us never see in the blurred hustle of life.

Thanks to some strategic social engineering by friends, Bruce and Hetty met for the first time a while after that. And, to no one's surprise who knew them both, they fell in love.

Bruce visited our home recently when he was in town for a performance. He was seated, barely, an elbow on each knee and leaning so far forward he looked as if he might at any minute bolt across the room and out the door. "It's not what I do," he was saying of acting. "It's who I *am*." He crouched still farther forward, nearly in a sprinter's position. "And the same is true for Hetty, for her art. It's who she *is*."

You and I both know the gleam in the eye, the lift in the voice, the uncontainable energy when you speak with someone who thinks of work as more than a paycheck or a title. You watch and listen and marvel and wonder if that person across the table from you might at any moment lift up on some unseen wings and soar skyward—leaving you to clear the plates.

I see this in my friend Mary Anne Severino, who nearly bounces in her seat when she talks about social work. Having graduated from Vanderbilt some years ago, she took time off to care for three children, the youngest of whom has just entered kindergarten. Now Mary Anne is pursuing her master's degree in social work and thrilled to be reengaging with these issues. Her professional calling has its roots in her own childhood; long before she had ever trained as a social worker or begun a journey of faith, she would carry *National Geographic* magazines from her parents' collection up to her room—and weep, she says, over the poverty she saw in them.

Mary Anne's passion for her career and for parenting intertwine. Though it is early in spring, she is already planning the service projects her kids will conduct this summer. Her love for her own kids helps drive her concern for children at risk. And the needs of families all around the Severinos—refugees from wars and from natural disasters—help remind Mary Anne's kids of what struggles so many other kids face. Perhaps Mary Anne's response to her own calling will help her kids live into theirs.

Pesky Practical Matters—Like Money

Most of us at some point, if not for all our lives, function in jobs simply because there are mouths to feed and music lessons to fund. For plenty of us, the "calling" piece of our lives lies outside the workplace.

From what I can see, easily awed as I am by the electronically proficient, my friend Elizabeth Rogers understands computers intimately, a kind of high-tech Dr. Dolittle communing with the machines. But she's insightful in clarifying the conclusion she's come to: the work her husband, Jason, does *is* a calling for him, and family is a calling for them both. Her paid job, though, is a helpful *skill* that provides income for the family. She feels fortunate to have a three-day-a-week schedule and marvelous co-workers. For her, though, the work she does contributes to the family's ability to provide for the kids—it isn't a calling in that gut sense of "deep gladness."

"And," she adds pointedly, "I need a midlife-crisis retreat every time you ask me these questions."

It's what we call Real Life: the necessity of jobs that provide for our families and the constant tension of wanting to be sure that at least some of our waking hours are spent on our driving passion and purpose.

For years Todd and I have asked each other the questions: *If money were no object, what would you get up and do every day? Is there a way we can structure our family life so you can do more of that?*

Now, unless Bill Gates shows up at Thanksgiving as our long-lost—and *much* beloved—uncle, money is and always will be an issue at our house. But for many of us, there *are* ways—if we have the courage and creativity—to restructure how we spend money and time so that either (1) work that is a *skill* can be limited timewise to allow for focus on our central callings, both family and other work, or (2) we might find ways to redirect our skills into areas that align more directly with our sense of calling and passion.

Doris Betts muses that for some of us, at least for some seasons, "maybe the calling has more to do with the *how* than the *what*. It's *how* you wait those tables, sell those shoes, rear a family, stay married…"

So the *how* of the work can become a purpose itself: a job—even one we might not have chosen had all our options been open—performed with dedication, perseverance, and kindness.

Or sometimes, as Doris Betts found for herself, having followed one's calling becomes more clear when gazing back over the years:

When I look back, this fifty-year marriage seems it was meant to be. At the time, I was swept away into marriage. Babies were born ahead of schedule; I felt less "called" than swept along by the currents. It takes time to remember that this was a way of life chosen, not just one you're swimming through.

It's worth paying attention to what we have chosen, and why, and what we've simply done because it was part of a duty that we tried to do well. Not just biding our time until the *real* journey begins, or the *real* destination's achieved, but counting even this day as a journey that matters—one that may, in fact, someday show itself to be part of our larger purpose.

Confessing Class Issues

Let me say quickly that economic and educational class issues have a tremendous impact on any discussion of calling. I'm painfully aware that most of the world, and particularly women, don't get to choose a profession any more than we choose where we're born: they simply struggle each day to survive and to help their children survive. United Nations figures show that globally 1.2 billion people earn less than one dollar a day and that the vast majority of the world's most desperately poor are women, constrained by limited access to education, job training, and financial resources. Worldwide, in fact, for all our flashy, twenty-first-century progress, the average woman earns just slightly more than *half* of the average man's wages.[5]

Worldwide, then, very few people get to muse over coffee with friends about how, in some distant tomorrow, they might shift careers or start a new business or cut back on hours for the sake of their kids. They do what they can, when and where and how they can, so that there will even *be* a tomorrow for them and their kids. So those of us who've stumbled into the luxury of education and the economic safety net that comes with that are in positions of tremendous privilege to begin with.

And if, like my friend Jennifer the dentist, you buy into the fairly scary New Testament idea that to whom much has been given, much shall be required,[6] you've taken on tremendous responsibility along with that privilege. Jennifer struggles with how the profession she loves aligns with her desire to assist people without access to dental care in her city. As it is, she has a regular pool of low-income patients she assists. But if money were no object? That's easy, she's quick to say:

> I'd work two to three days a week and volunteer my dentistry. There is so
> much need here…for dental care among the poor. I have found several

avenues to have these folks come to my office several times a week and I love it. I just wish money weren't even a part of dentistry and I could just do what I love without worrying about paying bills and saving for retirement.

Jennifer's someone who takes seriously her own sense of "deep gladness" *and* her knowledge that, as a highly educated white-collar woman, she most decidedly qualifies for the much-shall-be-required category. So she cobbles those insights together into work that pays bills, yes, a job that she's good at and loves, but also work that answers a need in the world around her.

Born into a Calling

For some, *calling* is a word reserved only for religious-specific work and for messages from God that arrive with blinding light or winged delivery boys. The prophet Isaiah, with his six-winged seraphim and his singed lips, had a calling. Jeremiah, poor man, bellowing from the bottom of a muddy pit, had a calling. Deborah, the Chief Justice of the Hebrew people who held court at her own Palm, the Palm of Deborah—she had a calling too. And so did Huldah, the Hebrew prophetess, and so did Dorcas, the seamstress whose fashions were all designed for the poor.

These were not extraordinary people handpicked for social polish or their skyscraper of an IQ. The prophets, in fact, weren't particularly well mannered or even marginally well liked. They complained to God of being unable to speak well, of being too young, too inexperienced, too fearful or shy, or too far from holy.

Too far from holy. Yet called. There's comfort in this, if we'll take it. There's also a challenge: to do something uncommon. Something hard. Something we're good at. Something, perhaps, born in us before we even knew it was there.

Shannon Sedgwick Davis, an attorney and a vice president of Geneva Global, a charitable-giving foundation that emphasizes performance philanthropy, describes herself as "humbled and fascinated that I should be so lucky, that just by showing up, I am given a divine opportunity to bring justice to so many suffering and dying around the world."

That passion to meet needs in the world, she says, has its roots in her own childhood:

I remember one trip my family took to Washington DC back when I was in middle school. We were outside a memorial, and there was this older woman who had a sign, protesting something.… Everyone was ignoring her, and that made me mad because she had something she needed to say. I approached her and began to discuss with her whatever it was that was upsetting her. I talked with her for an hour while my family toured the memorial. I've always wanted to fight for the underdog. To give a voice to those who have no voice.

Similarly, Gloria White-Hammond's sense of professional and personal calling can be traced to her childhood:

When I was around eight years old, I remember reading this blue book called *How to Become a Doctor* and deciding, "That's it! That's what I'll do!" Fortunately, I didn't have parents who said, "Are you crazy? Do you know that you're black and you're a girl? None of that stuff goes together."

Though Gloria's parents knew a different reality, they never discouraged her ambitions as a child,

so at no point along the way did it ever occur to me that I couldn't do it, which is really strange, because I never saw any physicians who were black, and certainly none who were women. Maybe that was just God's protection upon me.

As a pediatrician, Gloria is the person you call to check out carnival-colored rashes on your toddler's leg. As one of the pastors of an African Methodist Episcopal church, she is the person you consult on structuring effective Christian education for children. Among the nation's most innovative community leaders, Gloria and her husband, Ray Hammond (also a minister and a medical doctor), are the parents of two beautiful daughters and grandparents to a new granddaughter, and they're the people you invite to speak on how to reach urban youth.

But Gloria waves aside any image of herself as a spiritual, medical, or child-development guru and prefers to speak of her varied professional passions as simply following a calling, step by step.

In her own professional life, Gloria has learned to "take exception" to society's assumption that children raised in difficult circumstances will inevitably repeat the mistakes of their family or peer group. Part of that challenge gets lived out through an inner-city Boston pediatric clinic serving primarily Latinos and African Americans.

"Just really devoted families" is how she describes her patients. "The neighborhood has changed quite a bit," she notes, "because it's so heavily gentrified, but our families continue to come—sometimes a great distance. I still really love those people; I love the privilege of ministering in their lives.… It's the whole business of connecting." Pediatrics fits her well because, as she says,

> you get so involved with entire families.… That's just so special as a pediatrician, to be able to come alongside these families and touch them.… I've got some horror stories along the way as well, but…somebody has got to be there even then for them because…they need to be able to see somebody who connected with them even when they were in the gutter. And that's me.

The Callings We Try to Run From

Gloria's professional area of expertise has recently expanded to include a microenterprise development organization, My Sister's Keeper, which assists formerly enslaved Sudanese women—most of them violently abducted, many of them raped—with health care and loans for starting their own businesses. In one trip to Sudan alone, she and her group negotiated the liberation of well over a thousand of these women from slavery.[7] My Sister's Keeper has purchased a grinding mill to employ Sudanese women and girls and is building a new school to educate them.

"When I first went to Sudan," Gloria recalls, "I certainly would not have had it in my spirit to go back." In fact, she found encountering the extreme poverty utterly debilitating. "But I had this uncanny sense that I needed to go back, and as time went on, it was clear that this was the piece the Lord wanted me to take on."

And here's where the idea of calling has to include not only what we feel pulled toward early in life, or what we learn to accept we're good at, but also the unlikely, the unexpected, perhaps the highly undesirable things God seems to nudge us toward anyway, despite all our eloquent protests. Gloria points to her own childhood to contrast her personal tendencies with divine calling:

> I don't like getting dirty—I never did.... I didn't make mud pies as a kid because I didn't like to get dirty. And I don't like to eat chicken with my fingers because then your fingers get dirty. Dirt does not work for me. And of course here I am in Sudan: you can't bathe for four or five days, and when you do, you've got a little basin with a couple inches of water.... I don't like using nasty toilets...and of course in Sudan there *are* no toilets—it's a hole in the ground. Bugs fly in and bugs fly out while you're using it, so this cannot possibly be Gloria. I don't do bugs.
>
> So in all these areas, I'm taking on things, and encountering things, and getting through stuff that is very much not me as I've known me. I'd have to say, bottom line, it is really a sense of calling. It's not me. Definitely not me.

Gloria's life exemplifies two kinds of calling: the first, an early interest and affinity that remained constant and fit with who she was; the other coming later in life, developing, becoming clear only over time, and often answered with a certain reluctance, or even outright resistance:

> The only thing I was really sure of as a girl was that I was interested in medicine.... In terms of the ministry [including her work in Sudan], that clearly was a sense of calling that I was not looking to pursue, not asking God to direct me on that path. You know how this works: you hear the call and you try to figure out if there is enough room in the boat for you *and* Jonah.

And like the prophets before her, she's found some kinds of callings don't fit as much who you are as who God wants you to become *now*, in this particular season.

"I Know Nothing"

Over the years, I've been fortunate to hear novelist Bret Lott speak several times. Lott's novels are of a rare breed that when I assign one in a college class, I'm later assured by surprised students, "Dr. Jordan-Lake, I actually read it on the airplane over spring break and didn't even have to *make* myself finish it."

On more than one occasion, I've heard Lott read from an essay about his life just before one of his books, *Jewel*, was selected by Oprah's Book Club. He tells the story of sitting at a soccer game and bellowing to one of his sons to *Get in the game!* He is venting his frustration because his own work, his latest novel, is failing—a complete wreck, he's beginning to realize. And even as he is yelling, he recalls *Jewel*, the story about his own grandmother and the daughter with Down syndrome to whom his grandmother courageously devoted her life. At that soccer game, suddenly aware of his own behavior (his wife has scooted her own lawn chair quite a few feet away to distance herself), he demands of himself how he could have written of a parent's wisdom, patience, and sacrifices for a child and have learned nothing of parenting himself. It's a powerful essay, ending with the confession of all honest parents, *I know nothing, I know nothing, I know nothing* followed quickly by this: *I am blessed, I am blessed, I am blessed.*[8]

That's how it goes, doesn't it? That twin-engine sense of *I have been gifted*—or, if you're as bold as Flannery O'Connor, *I'm good at it*—together with *I know nothing*. And underlying it all, every moment, the bedrock nevertheless of it all: *I am blessed, I am blessed, I am blessed.*

For me, the *I know nothing* comes from within, the constant voice that tells me to doubt myself in all things, including my choice of tea at Starbucks and my choice of chapter arrangement and whether or not I'm a really big fool or only a medium-sized one for trying to be a writer. Or a professor. Or a good mother. Or a good wife.

For the *I'm good at it*, I can thank a circle of kind and generous family and friends—but most especially my husband.

Partners in Pursuit of Calling

Todd and I are case studies in extremes, which makes for an E-ticket ride of a marriage. Though not prideful, he possesses an unwavering sense of who he is and what he's about. I admire the trait, except for the times I'm ramming, horns down, up against it. And even then, I envy it.

I, on the other hand, find not only God's mercies, compassion, and faithfulness new morning by morning, but also my capacity to be *completely* convinced that I won't be able to accomplish a single worthwhile thing that day. Which throws me back on the mercies and compassion of God.

But from one point of the spectrum to the other, my husband to me, we could *all* use support and affirmation, especially from the people dearest to us.

It's easier to be single and pursue this idea of calling and passion in your work and your personal life than it is to be married to someone who wants you to play things safe: *by all means, don't rock the boat.* Not that such a spouse is a bad person. There are financial responsibilities, mouths to feed, mortgages to pay. These are, of course, valid concerns. and ones you'll be arrested for neglecting.

It's just harder, once you're Married with Children, to follow your heart into uncharted lands *if* your spouse has no desire, thanks very much, to leave the Land of the Safe and Secure, too.

But there are seasons when God asks us to run after more than just safety and a big paycheck. To have a partner in that run is valuable beyond measure. If your spouse not only recognizes the ways in which God has gifted you but also prods you and comforts you and challenges you, and expects the same in return, well, *that* is buttressing you can build on.

To have your life partner be that gentle-strong whisper above, as poet T. S. Eliot put it, "the voices singing in our ears, saying / That this was all folly,"[9] to have a spouse who reminds you who you are and all you can be, why, this is precious indeed.

When the Spirit Tugs on Your Sleeve

That's not to say there are always Happily Ever After endings. The Princess Finding Her Way to the Palace Permanently is Disney's shtick. It just doesn't happen to be real life.

Real life is, though, all about grace. Grace is the thing that meets us at the beginning, when we're scared to leave the dock because, as surely everyone else knows, we're not really so good at this. That's when grace climbs on board with us.

Sometimes life is about launching out simply because you're driven to do it, although clearly it's not the safest or the most sensible move—and you didn't bring the right shoes. Grace pushes us out from the very real perils of sitting quietly, calmly, there in the slip.

There simply are no guarantees what pursuing a calling will cost. But then, that would be the point of adventure. And faith.

Sometimes it's about listening to the dreams and hopes you had as a child, what you thought you could do before the Big Bad Wolf of a world came and blew your house down and told you that you couldn't.

Sometimes it's about paying attention—not to what you feel comfortable doing, but to what you've never felt comfortable doing and yet still feel compelled to pursue: drawn, pulled, sometimes even dragged on some invisible cord sewn securely to your insides.

Despite all the dirt. And the bugs.

Sometimes, God tugs on your sleeve *because* of those things. And won't leave you alone. Pulls on your pant leg. Taps your shoulder.

When my son, Justin, was little and couldn't get my attention, he'd plant himself in my path and put his request this way: "Mommy, turn your face around."

Which, I think, is how God often calls: waiting—beside us or right there up ahead—saying our names and waiting...until we turn our faces around.

Spectators on Shore

Dealing with Others' Opinions of
Your Work and Family Decisions

I t can't be done," was where the conversation ended.

This book had just been through the fires of the editorial board. Editorial board, as I understand it, means that a group of smart, savvy, and politely ruthless people gather around a table while one of them, the acquisitions editor—who is the writer's dragon slayer, therapist, and first name on the acknowledgments page—presents why your book should be published.

It was the day after one particularly invincible acquisitions editor had convinced her publisher to let this particular book live. Our family had been invited for lunch with another family we were just getting to know. Todd, being the world's finest unpaid publicist, was barely across their threshold before he began waxing eloquent in his best Proud Spouse kind of way about my upcoming book contract.

The couple exclaimed politely over the news—as required by the unpaid publicist's emphatic Italian hand motions and dramatic pauses. They graciously held out their arms for our coats.

Then Todd offered the subject of the book.

This was a mistake.

"Two careers and kids?" our host asked. "I can tell you one thing about that."
We all waited. I glanced around for pen and paper, in case this called for notes.
"I can tell you," he said. "It can't be done."
"You mean…," my husband began.
"I mean *it can't be done.*"
For a moment I thought he was kidding.
He wasn't kidding.
I did not take notes.

At first I reacted in the courageous way I always do to criticism: by telling myself all the ways this person was right. Not only was the premise of this book ludicrous, so was the idea of being a writer. Who did I think I was anyway? Being a writer, and therefore an artistic type of personality—which means that no sane person should have to live with me—I tend to get just a little discouraged between books or between affirming e-mails from my agent. By a little discouraged I mean that I'm certain I'm infringing on everyone else's air by breathing.

And the truth is—if you'll pinky-promise not to breathe a word of this to my host—that on some days I've agreed with him, and worse, I've thought this book should be whole chapters of blank pages followed by the afterword: *Aaaaggghhh!* There are days and there are nights when the demands of sick children and unvaccinated dogs and staff meetings and science-fair projects take all the spunk and conscious thought out of me. Some days it's not even the lack of time so much as the thousand-points-of-shopping-list sludge that clogs the lobes of the brain. I try to be aware that there's a humanitarian crisis in Sudan where my friend Gloria is helping build schools for women and girls—but all I can hear in my head is: *Barney or Elmo Pull-Ups? Snickers or suckers for the middle-school treat bags? Is there a product that removes Silly Putty from hair?* And I want to throw up my arms and surrender: "It's true. It *can't* be done."

But this is where one of my worst traits comes into play: stubbornness. As I pound away at my keyboard, trying to carve out a life in which two people try to listen to God and use their gifts and nurture their children, my own lug-headed determination keeps me going. Work is too good and family too precious and gifts too important for us to give up on making it all come together. So this chapter is a cry of defiance that no matter how we steer our lives, no matter how we respond season by season to the beautiful tension of work and family, we cannot let *can't* be the last word. No matter what others say.

When Everyone Has an Opinion

The reality is that the very act of raising children seems to invite everyone to offer perspectives on the ways you do and—quite obviously—do *not* balance career and family.

And as far as I can tell, women are particularly subject to criticism and particularly sensitive to these voices. It is somehow our fault if a toddler is too aggressive ("too much day care," people whisper) or a sixth grader is too shy ("too much homeschooling," they shake their heads) or dust bunnies set up camp on our living room floors ("she works outside the home, you know"). With both the womb-births of my first two children and the heart-birth adoption of the third, I wondered if I had a sign on my back that said How's My Parenting? with a number to call—mine—for reporting sightings of misconduct.

No doubt about it: it's not fair. But as my friend Ginger, who can be counted on for both bear hugs and big kicks in the behind, likes to say, "So now what're ya gonna *do* about it?"

Perhaps the time I was most aware of plowing headlong into everyone's disapproval was when my husband and I made the decision to leave Boston and move to the rural outskirts of Charlotte, North Carolina. Now I'm not saying the town didn't have its charms; I loved it, and the people were gems. It's just that the Feed and Seed at the crossroads was the hot spot of town center.

My friends in the English Department at Tufts worried that I didn't have a job lined up yet; I was following my husband.

My friends at my church worried we were leaving congregation-based ministry for university work.

A sophisticated, urbane German friend who passed through the little town where we'd bought a house called us from a phone booth on the main street. Appalled at what she saw, she nearly hyperventilated over the line.

Friends who knew we'd be taking a 40 percent drop in family income worried over our finances.

Some friends, especially women friends, worried I'd have too little work outside the home.

Some friends, especially women friends, worried I'd be up to my usual tricks and take on too much.

Everyone had an opinion: I should cut back on work. I should ramp up. I should finish my doctorate quickly, before I slipped into that Slough of Despond, the Land of the All but Dissertation. I should not finish the doctorate at all but stay home and behave. I should have finished the doctorate yesterday, before I even began thinking of letting children slow down the pace.

Friends and onlookers let us know: We should stay. We should go. We should sell our quirky old farmhouse with the great view out the back to them.

Some people, I think, just covered their eyes with their hands and held their breath and prayed.

And it isn't the last time everyone will be heard from—in my life or yours. But I learned something about sifting through voices: it's important to distinguish between those who are merely venting or speaking out of their own disappointments and those who know us and love us and have our family's best interest in mind—even if that runs counter to what they *wish* we would do.

Navigating Our Mothers

Jennifer, my dentist friend in Texas, recently e-mailed about having to interview new employees in her own home because she'd just given birth. And because of the timing, she interviewed them while she was nursing. What's a woman—and a dentist in private practice—to do when the office is shrieking for help and the baby is too? Whether the two new employees thought, *You go, girl!* or something less nice, I'm guessing they nodded and smiled—if they wanted the job. So I'll say it myself: *You go!*

But apparently *all of us* trying to navigate these waters find them full of lots and lots of free-floating opinions, some sharp enough to split you wide open. For women, the approval—or not—of our own mothers and mothers-in-law may be the most threatening. And sometimes, too, the most wise.

Linguist Deborah Tannen, author of the bestselling *You Just Don't Understand,* recently published her study of mother-daughter relations, *You're Wearing THAT?* Mothers and daughters spend more time talking than mothers and sons or fathers and daughters or fathers and sons: thus the possibilities not only for mother-daughter connection but also for misunderstandings are immense.[1]

A brilliant young British woman in my church in New England once confessed to our small group on a retreat that she was just beginning to realize that she'd so aggressively pursued her education because her mother used to tell her she was stupid. She had spent her life trying to prove her mother wrong, graduating from Cambridge and then finishing a doctorate at Harvard. To those of us on the outside, she'd turned her insecurities into a killer résumé. But the look of pain in her eyes spoke of oceans of hurt that she'd had to learn, by faith, to cross. She's a mother now herself, and though we've lost touch, I'm certain she makes a point of affirming her children.

My friend Jane Tan, a physician who also holds a PhD, explains that her own response to work and motherhood is "inextricably linked" with her own childhood and her own mother:

> She was highly educated, but after having children and moving to another country, she was forced to give up her career and stay at home. I think that because of this, she transferred her own ambitions and goals onto us too much to allow room for a healthy parent-child relationship.... By the grace of God, we have developed a better, new relationship, but my mother still struggles with issues of self-worth and self-esteem.
>
> As a mother, there was no doubt in my mind that continuing to work full time was the right choice for me. Knowing my own goal-oriented and ambitious nature, I knew that I would run the same risk of feeling empty once my children are grown and that I would hover over them a little too much otherwise. I am happy with the decision that I have made, and every week starts with an internal examination of whether I have a reasonably balanced life.

My own mother offered unwavering support of her children as we grew. So theoretically, I have no excuse for near-paralyzing bouts of insecurity and indecision.

But whether we come by our insecurities honestly or unpredictably, I'm here to tell you: left to run wild, they'll destroy you.

"We break our backs," my friend Gloria likes to say, "in order to keep up our fronts."

"Amen," her congregation calls back. "You know *that's* right."

Me, too. I want a bumper sticker made of it.

But any career/family decision women make that differs from that of the older women around us can seem like an implied rejection of the very real sacrifices the women who taught us how to be women once made. It's nothing short of gunpowder leaking loose from the barrels; we mothers and grandmothers and daughters dance around it with torches and try not to trip.

One of the senior members of my extended family gave me this gift of a revelation one day: "When I was pregnant with my first child," she mused, "I was a secretary and hated my job. My job meant nothing to me. I couldn't wait to quit work to stay home. I think it's different for your generation."

I wanted to drop to my knees in thanksgiving. "Yes!" I felt like shouting. "Yes, that's the difference exactly."

Because no matter what a modern mother decides at different seasons of her child-rearing life, once she's been out in the working world where her ideas are valued, where her contributions get rewarded with direct deposits, where her education or talent gets put to use, it's no easy step to have her lunch meetings restricted to joints with a PlayPlace and have her suggestions boxed into the realms of *I do believe it's nap time.* Even—and this is important—even when that's what she's willingly chosen for this season.

They say that "the hand that rocks the cradle rules the world." (My middle-school daughter would revise that to *rocks the world.*) The longer I'm a mother myself, the more I believe that, and the more I respect the rich insight and the strength of the women who've come before me. The more I respect the precious gift—and the power—of motherhood. The more I remember to cherish this day, this developmental stage of childhood, this tree painted on the wallpaper, even this mess and this muddle, because it turns out that it's true what they try to tell us as new parents: you cannot go back. It once sounded to me like a criticism, a threat, a warning to stay home and hush. Now I understand it to be a wisdom held out for the taking from older parents who desperately want you to know: what seems like an eternity of long nights and lost sleep strung together in a blur of too many coffee-fueled days will quickly turn to kissing good-bye at a dorm room. I see now that these gray-haired parents risk seeing you bristle because the stakes of potential regret are so high.

Learning to Sift Through Advice

Attorney Shannon Sedgwick Davis, whose charitable foundation work takes her all over the world, recalls that when people learned she was expecting and that she didn't plan on resigning her job, she met with "snickers, and a whole lot of criticism." Noting that although her family comes first, she also insisted, "God created me with this passion [for my work]. God called me to this, and God hasn't called me away." With the help of a nanny, she works out of her home, where she can take conference calls and conduct research but also hear when Connor, just learning to walk, takes a fall. Her husband, Sam, has cut back on his professional hours so that the whole family can travel together when needed.

Peggy Wehmeyer is a top-flight broadcast journalist, for seven years ABC's religion correspondent for *World News Tonight, 20/20,* and *Good Morning America,* and now a full-time spokesperson for World Vision International. This is a woman who has interviewed George W. Bush, Bill Clinton, Billy Graham, and Muhammad Ali, among others.

With wit and authenticity, she tells of the opposition she met along the way. Wehmeyer came to faith as a college student and then became passionate about the "truth-telling" demands of journalism that seemed to match her newfound spiritual purpose; she started her career thinking she would pursue a profession in full-time religious work. But when doors began to open for her in secular broadcast media, a Christian leader told her that if she proceeded down the professional road she'd begun, she would surely (a) lose her faith and (b) find that no Christian man would want to marry her, since she'd be far too threatening.

A couple of decades later, now a wife, a mother of two, and a well-respected, sought-after professional whose intelligence, integrity, and faith principles are widely known, Wehmeyer spoke at the commencement ceremony of Gordon

College. "I would never tell you to ignore wise counsel," she said, "but you must trust your own deepest convictions and not let anyone else overwhelm the quiet pull of God on your life. You're the one who will be coming home every day to your choices."[2]

When I spoke with her once in person, the two of us trotting along in pumps back to her bed-and-breakfast so she could hustle back up I-35 to Dallas in time for the next engagement, she spoke of her sense of professional calling with a confidence I wish came in capsule form. And she spoke of professional sacrifices she'd made for her family life, including refusing to move to New York and refusing a journalistic assignment to Jerusalem, the latter having decidedly damaged her career.

"But that's okay," she was quick to add. "I have no regrets."

At the time, her children were attending a private school in which the vast majority of other mothers were not working outside the home. Which led her to speak of a willingness to be different. And letting God be the center of whatever it is you do.

Both Peggy and Shannon have listened to those around them but remained firm when others tried to shake their resolve in how they were navigating kids and career.

"I've just felt," Shannon said simply, "like God called me to both."

Sometimes Conflicted

My husband and I were in the final paperwork stages of adding our third child. This is the time in the adoption process that a real face of a real child appears on your computer screen—like a biological child's ultrasound, only excruciating for the adoptive parent because you can't be physically present with the little one that has already become *your child. Yours.*

Soon after seeing my daughter's picture, I received an e-mail from a colleague who knew we were in the process of adopting. She suggested in strong terms that every child needed a stay-at-home mother, one who would surrender all her own selfish—okay, she didn't *say* selfish, but she implied it—goals for the sake of her child. I was dead wrong to bring a child, even one life-sentenced to an orphanage, into our family if I couldn't give her full-time, at-home care.

Her message exploded in my spare little office. Shaken, I sent a reply that was vulnerable, honest—and porcupined with defensiveness. I explained that I habitually made sacrifices for my children, including teaching only part time so that I could write part time late at night, which probably worked out to less than the minimum wage—I've never let myself do the math—so that I could spend time with my kids, stay home when they were sick, sled with them on snow days, and be there for every last blasted My-Kid-Is-the-Second-Squash-from-the-Left school skit. My husband has been an *incredible* dad, I went on, who performed back handsprings with his work schedule so that he could be there for the kids and so that I could have more time to write and to teach. Perhaps she'd not known that...

But no sooner had I pounded the Send key than I sniffed a traitor—and it was inside my own skin. I think therapists call this *conflicted*. How could I be so defensive of my own decisions and at the same time so staunchly supportive of my colleagues who had less flexible work hours than mine? In my own rush to justify my life, I'd distanced myself from people I knew were doing a superb job of parenting. I'd popped off at this woman because she'd pressed my independent, don't-be-telling-me-what-to-do buttons, even though I struggled myself with those very questions. *Could* we respond to the needs of an infant, in addition to the demands of two older children and two professional callings?

From my office, I e-mailed my friend Kelly Shushok, a mother and part-time professional. I pasted in my colleague's message but left out her name—my only classy act of the day.

On a subject of an everyday nature, Kelly can take days to reply. On this kind of thing, though, nanoseconds come into play.

And there it was, sure enough, an immediate reply: "I'd say Ms. Omniscient Budinski owes you a fair sight more than an apology—like, for example, her first-born child—no, wait: I'm guessing she doesn't *have* children, which would of course make her an expert on *yours!*"

A friend of this vindictiveness on your behalf is not to be lost.

To be fair, my colleague did apologize, profusely and graciously. But it still stung, both her unsolicited scolding and, maybe more so, my own reaction—an uptight, knee-jerk response that exposed my own worries.

We did radically reshape our family life once again several months later for the sake of our third child. But I'd like to think our slowing and turning the ship was less due to an outsider's well-meaning pronouncements than it was a result of listening to God and to a new rhythm of life.

Even Slow Learners Can Learn

I'm a slow learner, but I'm coming to understand that focusing on what purpose God has in mind for my life can be something I rest in—the buttressing that keeps my flimsy lean-to of a life from collapsing in the first rain. And I've learned a lot about prayer.

I say this carefully, not glibly, because so many religious types throw out the "I'll pray about that" line like a life preserver tossed overboard with no rope connecting it to the ship. But there truly *are* ways to pray for guidance and get it. These are not the *I'll-know-God-wants-me-to-resign-from-this-job-if-the-light-turns-green...now* prayers. That's called superstition. We've all tried it, and it doesn't work—or we'd try it again. I'm talking about the grueling, in-silence, heart-ripped-open, fasting-from-food-and-cell-phone-and-e-mail kind of prayer, over time.

Now I was raised Baptist, and despite my best efforts to add linen to my wardrobe and liturgy to my worship, I have somehow never managed the move to a Christian tradition that would offer a deeper, richer tradition of prayer and meditation and better architecture, like the Episcopalians, the Catholics, the Quakers. We Baptists do action verbs well, though not so much being silent or waiting or sitting-still listening. For us Baptists to pursue prayer and silence and meditation and fasting—*please no, not fasting!*—is like a Chihuahua taking a vow of silence.

But it *can* be done. Over time. With room for error and a keen memory of past mistakes and lessons learned from them. Seeking God's wisdom. God's guidance. God's timing. Lots of holy-sounding categories that, it turns out, really matter in trying to live a life of meaning and purpose season by season.

The key is keeping your eyes on God and handpicking the spectators you'll listen to. Spectators may or may not have a clue as to what's going on in your life or where God might be leading you. Or sometimes, I've learned the hard way, you may not have a clue yourself what's going on in your life—the human capacity for self-delusion being truly astounding. So having some voices nearby that you trust is essential, both for the encouraging word and that spine-rattling *Are you really so wrapped up in other things not to see...*

In real life, keeping our eyes on God rarely—okay, never—means watching for a biplane with a message in the sky. More often it means steering a boat in the dusk with only some buoys and a vague map. But even to the chronically uncertain like me, God offers a kind of gut-level assurance—enough light in the dark to navigate by, a way out from the shoals where we've foundered—when we're watching and listening and paying attention.

So you and I, we've got to keep our eyes on the only One who can tell us when to lower the anchor and when to hoist all the sails and when we need to quit being so scared of the storm.

And when to toss all the *can'ts* overboard before they rot in the sun and smell the place up.

Charting the Course as You Go

Navigating by Grace

A re you a little unclear on the best way to chart the course so that you can achieve professionally all you were born to do *and* have meaningful relationships with stable, happy kids and a spouse whose work is also fulfilling?

See if you can find a pattern in the following people's professional paths:

- When Corazon Aquino applied for the presidency of her country, the Philippines, she filled in the blank for vocation with this: housewife. She had a good education and was multilingual and had intended to go to law school but got married instead. Her primary job experience? Raising five children. Which, as it turned out, served her well, along with a devout faith, in healing her violence-torn country.

- Before Rich Stearns became the executive director of the international humanitarian organization World Vision, which serves eighty-five million people in nearly one hundred countries, he was the CEO of the china and crystal manufacturing giant Lenox and was living with his wife and five kids in a ten-bedroom—yep, ten-bedroom—home. Before *that,* he'd been, by his own admission, a fairly condescending young man who'd insisted to his fiancée that they shouldn't pick out china and crystal patterns for their wedding, since such things were so terribly materialistic.

- Before Madeleine Albright—who would become the United States' first female secretary of state—was thirty-nine, she'd never held a paid professional position. Like Aquino, she had education in her favor. She was also a polyglot, fluent in French and Czech with a passable knowledge of Russian, Polish, German and Serbo-Croatian. But her primary employment had been raising three daughters. Which, she's been known to joke, prepared her perfectly to be Madame Secretary, insisting that world leaders "play well together."

- Before she began the work that became her life's passion, Mairead Corrigan Maguire had little in the way of breathtaking academic or professional credentials. She'd not been a head of state or an international diplomat. No management experience. No strategic climbing of a corporate ladder. She'd been a secretary. But because of a national tragedy that devastated her own family, she was catapulted into the political realm. For the ways in which she turned personal crisis into a pivotal moment in the history of Northern Ireland, she was awarded the Nobel Peace Prize.

- After Ray Hammond earned his undergraduate degree from Harvard, he earned a master's degree in Middle Eastern languages, then went on to medical school, became a surgeon, and began raising two daughters with his pediatrician wife. Today he's a prominent African Methodist Episcopal pastor as well as a leading civic voice in Boston and around the country.

- Zealous about prosecuting child abusers and assisting in the children's healing, Beth Toben is an assistant district attorney. And a mother. And married to the dean of a law school. But long before any of that, she hadn't ever planned on going to law school. In fact, she initially enrolled only because her father insisted on it to help her recover from a broken engagement.

- The son of an international diplomat, Marcus Hummon grew up in Africa, Europe, Southeast Asia, and the Middle East. A strong student, he might have made a fine diplomat himself. Instead, with no southern or country music credentials, he became a country songwriter-musician. In the late nineties, though, he lost his record-company contract and thought he'd failed at the one thing he'd always wanted to do. This was when he finally allowed his agent to sell his songs for other artists to sing. And this was when his songs, including "God Bless the Broken Road," became hits—with Wynonna Judd, Tim McGraw, Rascal Flatts, and Kathy Mattea, among others. Along the way, he took theology classes at Vanderbilt Divinity School, where he met future wife, Becca Stevens. Together they would have three children. Becca would become Vanderbilt's Episcopal chaplain and the founder of Magdalene House, a thriving ministry providing jobs, a caring community, and housing for former prostitutes. And Marcus would begin writing opera and musical theater.

Having trouble discerning a pattern for the best way to chart your course? *Precisely.*

Like a journey of faith, the course of raising children and following a professional calling and supporting a spouse in his or her professional calling can't be charted ahead of time. At best, you simply make clear your commitments and your intended direction—and *go*.

Still, lots of us, early in our adult lives, look about hopefully, waiting for someone to hand us a map in glossy full color from Princess Cruises that explains how our journey will include these four pleasant ports, a ship that stays on top of the water, and shipmates who chew with their mouths closed.

Life just doesn't happen that way.

Which is the best and the worst news we could get.

You Can't Chart Too Far Ahead

One thing I've learned after three children, more than three fine lines of aging, and even more job changes, is that you can't chart every season and storm and full-sail run when you're standing on the dock. It looks a lot easier from shore, with no complexities, no financial disasters, no birth defects, no separations or layoffs.

And it sounds a lot simpler when there aren't yet any powerful currents of parental devotion that can knock us clear off our professional feet.

One of my favorite graduate-school colleagues, Sarah Hanselman, liked to say that I should be a poster child for the campaign that "Even You, Yes, *You*, May Have Latent Maternal Instincts." She watched me transition from a nauseous, anxious, remarkably enlarged pregnant woman strategizing just how *many* hours of child care I could afford to a goofily beaming, gradually shrinking mother calculating how *few* hours of child care I could get by with.

"I tried to tell you," she told me, as we leaned over the cradle where my first baby was in full air-band performance—mouth, head, arms, and legs all going at once. I could've sworn she was having "Sweet Home Alabama" piped into her crib.

"I know, I know," I admitted. "I just didn't…know."

She nodded. "How can you? Who could imagine?"

How can you indeed? Among my closest circle of friends and among the people I've interviewed over the years are women who never expected to want to quit their jobs after children, and did. Women who expected to have children once they'd reached their professional pinnacle, and couldn't. Women who expected to love staying home full time, and didn't. And men who'd been indifferent about whether they had children or not, only to turn their careers upside down just to spend more time at home with a baby. Some of these people balanced work and children spectacularly well—until the birth of a second child or a child with special needs sent the family life into new, unforeseen territory. Some worked long, hard hours through their children's infancy only to shift career tracks to a less demanding schedule when the children reached their teen years.

It's a journey you simply can't chart too far out ahead, and sometimes you can't see your own sails for the fog closing in. Which is where keeping a tight grip on faith comes in. And lots of late-night, heart-to-heart talks as a couple.

Good News and Bad News

I once approached a well-known speaker and writer to tell her I appreciated an essay of hers I'd just read. She thanked me, and somehow our conversation wended its way to professional women who also had children. At some point, she mentioned she'd just become a grandmother, and I told her how *terrific* she looked—saying this both because all women know this is what we must say and also because it was true.

"I tell the young women in universities I speak to," she added, "that they ought to marry and have children early and *then* get on with their careers."

I stood there trying to recall if I'd already mentioned the young ages of my kids and wondering if she could tell how not-terribly-young-anymore I was. Was this the rebuke that it seemed? I suddenly liked her essay less. And her skin didn't look quite as fresh and dewy as it had originally.

In retrospect, though, I don't believe she was being malicious so much as reflecting on what had worked well for her. It just doesn't happen to be a set of instructions I'd want to give anyone else: to marry and have children early, as if we could arrange these things at will.

Some years ago, I interviewed Secretary of Labor Elaine Chao. After jumping through the fifty-three-hundred official government hoops, it was a little startling to find an actual person, a genuine and likable woman, on the other end of the phone. The oldest of six daughters in a Chinese immigrant family, her résumé is a gathering of all the best schools, then a glittering lineup of leadership roles at the United Way and the Red Cross, followed by becoming the first Asian American woman to hold a presidential cabinet post. When she speaks to groups of young women or girls, she told me, she stresses that they should not "find a portion of themselves in someone else." It wasn't until her late thirties that she herself met her "soul mate," as she calls her husband, Senator Mitch McConnell. Like many of her former classmates from Harvard Business School, trying to have children after they'd established themselves professionally became a "race against the [biological] clock. Life has its trade-offs," she added. "That's important to know."

When Sylvia Ann Hewlett wrote about the increasing numbers of women who earn more than fifty thousand dollars a year who are childless, her book, *Creating a Life: Professional Women and the Quest for Children,* caused shock waves among those claiming never to have understood that waiting until later in life to try to conceive might mean you never get pregnant. My mother's generation understood this, and so did my grandmother's—but my generation has learned that waiting until later in life to pursue a career is also a risk. It can be done, and wondrously well. But, as with the opposite choice, there are no guarantees.

My friend Elizabeth Rogers's mother has had several separate careers since she raised her children, and at age sixty-one she finished her doctorate. What great spunk. I'm not sure, though, that I could've done the same thing or even pursued more education once my kids were in school. Graduate school was grueling enough when it was nearly done and the kids began to arrive. But with three children in live-action motion, I may never have finished—I probably would have fallen asleep on the keyboard with *Jay Jay the Jet Plane* bounding away in the background.

The *good news* is that there's no one-size-fits-all solution for planning your life—sorting work hours or child-care providers or taking time off from a career. There is no plastic Play-Doh presser into which every parent and child must be stuffed and squeezed out the right shape. Every family—and every individual child's needs—differs. Various careers lend themselves differently to flexing, working from home, finding on-site child care. And different seasons of life might include decreasing one or both spouses' hours or bringing children along on the job or finding baby-sitters you simply adore—the kind whose dating relationships and all other employment prospects you absolutely must sabotage lest they develop too much of a life outside your children.

Every family's solution will be tailor-made, season by season. Which brings us to the *bad news:* there's no one-size-fits-all solution. There's no money-back guarantee that if a mother drops out of the work force until all her little ones enroll in middle school, and then a father works part time through the teen years to ensure the kids are playing all the right sports and hanging with all the right crowd and cruising none of the wrong Internet sites, each child will turn out to be a stable, secure, contributing member of society whose IQ exceeds 150 and who never forgets Mother's Day.

So here's what I love about maintaining flexibility in one's career-and-kids marriage: you can be creative and make it up as you go.

And here's what I hate: being creative and making it up as you go.

It all comes of the good news that there are so many options these days for parents and children and professional life. Which is also the bad news: lots of decisions to make.

Because that means the burden falls to us to listen to God and to look at our lives and to make what our culture calls "good choices," which I gather from my middle-school daughter covers everything from saying no to methamphetamine to saying yes to eating your broccoli.

The choices can be paralyzing, especially when we believe the lie that we can control the future. Because the truth is, all we know is the situation at hand and roughly where we want to go. What decision can we make today that is in line with our intentions—and the intentions we believe God has for us? What would *work* for our family right now? What is *not* working, despite the encouragement or opinions of others? And we make changes or press on as we are, not because we can see the future, but because we can see what is in front of us—the good, the bad, the beautiful, and the frightening—and we take the next step.

Rough Water Ahead

Years ago, back when Todd and I were still discovering how to be married ourselves, we were conducting premarital counseling for couples in our Cambridge, Massachusetts, church.

One couple, Cathy and Kevin, were both earning doctorates in nuclear physics at MIT. They assured us that they could hardly communicate on a professional level, however, so different were their fields. It's a universal fact that we non-science types are a little cowed by the world of split atoms and light speed, so Todd and I nodded as if this made perfect sense. Clearly, it made no sense at all. This part I did understand, though: they wanted to be sure that they could at least communicate in their marriage, and they wanted to start out right—which they did.

They were also realistic enough to see the rough water ahead. Cathy knew she wanted children eventually and that she'd like to stay home for a while. She also knew what the track record of dedicated parents in her field looked like. Mommy-Track types ended up more Mommy than Track. Just keeping up with the latest discoveries in her field demanded one's full-time attention, so taking any time off meant falling far behind.

Other couples we counseled faced similar challenges—Man-Wah and Jane, for example, who had more education between them than whole counties where I come from. The job market was tight for two academics, even of their caliber. Whose job would they move for if the same school couldn't hire them both?

Clint Hinote was a graduate of the Air Force Academy and in the midst of finishing a graduate degree at Harvard's John F. Kennedy School of Government. Everything was on track for him to be a fine air force pilot, which would mean doing what he'd always wanted to do—and would also mean moving every couple of years. But during that mass dating event at our church that we church leaders naively called the coffee-doughnut fellowship hour, he'd met Myra Rubiera, who was a bright, ambitious Wellesley student considering going on for a doctorate in physics—and who was actively campaigning for the presidential candidate Clint was most decidedly *not* voting for. Love conquering all, he went with her to rallies and sheepishly carried her signs.

But Myra asked me to lunch and launched in right away: Clint's air force career would mean his moving often. What would happen to her professional ambitions, to the gifts God seemed to have given her, if she and Clint were to marry?

I thought of Myra just last week as I chatted with my neighbor Eliza. I've gotten to know Eliza's husband, Dana, since he's home often and works out in the yard. We trade compliments on each other's gracefully aging golden retrievers. And once his magazine for gourmet cooks landed in my mailbox—clearly, *that* wasn't mine. But it turns out that until just a few years ago, Eliza had been the traditional military wife, a stay-at-home mom involved with organizing the other families on base. Their family had lived all over the world. Then Dana retired, still young, and took a more flexible job so Eliza could go back to school. She's a neurologist now. The boys are in high school, excelling in music and soccer and, from what I can see, quite proud of their mom. Seasons of life...

So Myra, capable as my neighbor Eliza of becoming most anything, was understandably asking the same questions so many young adults ask: Do his/her career needs conflict with mine? How does proximity to extended family fit into all this? What if someday someone's parents begin to age and they need help? And what if the jobs are on the opposite coast? What if...?

What if, indeed.

Which is where trust comes in. Trust that God will be with us even in the *what-if.* Trust that God will work through us in ways we'd never have planned ourselves—even when we step out of the predictable.

From Model to Bishop

The career path of one prominent preacher I interviewed made me snicker, and she laughed even louder, both of us nearly spilling hot tea all over the table. Not every bishop of the African Methodist Episcopal denomination starts out as a broadcast journalist or spends seven years as a fashion model along the way. But then, Vashti Murphy McKenzie hasn't tracked her life along the lines of what's expected. Except, she will quickly point out, the women in her family did phenomenal things with their lives—long before women were supposed to.

"You were expected to *do something....* There was a sense of your place in history," she told me.

Conversations at the dinner table on Sundays ranged from economics to faith to civil rights. "My generation," she recalls, "had to prove ourselves."

Beginning her professional life in print journalism, Vashti found that her late-night deadlines began to clash with her NBA player–husband's schedule.

> He'd be returning from having been away for two weeks, and I'd be saying, "Could you have one of the guys bring you home from the airport? I'm on deadline." I knew I needed to back off from work. We were committed to each other. There was a sense of "I'll support you in whatever you do, and you support me in whatever I do." The [career] of an NBA player is much shorter than a reporter's, so I started to model. It was convenient.

She chuckled with me over the improbability of a fashion model being called to preach—and then becoming the first woman AME bishop. "But you know, it was God preparing me. I was very shy as a kid. A pastor can't be shy. And you can't be shy on a runway. I had to learn to be comfortable in crowds."

In Vashti's case, the plan had always been to "take [her] place in history." For the *how* and the *where* of doing that, she had to address each season as it came and adjust accordingly. And in retrospect, see God's leading even in the unlikely.

Tsunamis of the Unexpected

Maybe someday we'll realize that life rarely goes as we planned—and God shows up there too.

Nobel laureate Mairead Corrigan Maguire is a petite, unassuming woman. Her résumé, before that small detail of the Nobel Peace Prize, declared nothing extraordinary. Born in Belfast, Northern Ireland, to a window-cleaning contractor and a homemaker, she attended a commercial college for one year and became a secretary. Nothing in the early map of her life indicated she was headed for international recognition. Even now, her smile is soft and affable—not someone you would pick out of a crowd as liable to stare down armed violence and stand the world on its head.

Mairead's life course radically changed tack in the wake of a bloody tragedy. Her sister, Anne Maguire, and Anne's children were hit by an IRA getaway car whose driver had been shot by a British soldier. Three of the children died. Anne herself never recovered emotionally and later took her own life. Together with Betty Williams, Mairead helped mobilize Northern Ireland against sectarian violence. In response to the two women's efforts, tens of thousands turned out for marches demanding an end to the conflict—Catholics walking side by side with Protestants.

Several years after the tragedy, Mairead married Jackie Maguire, her deceased sister's husband, and helped raise the surviving three children. Mairead and Jackie also had two children of their own. In speaking with me, she was firm about babies needing to be home with a parent, though she said that during the years the children were small she'd continued her work in peace efforts by waiting until her husband got home from his job so she could slip out to her meetings.[1]

One of the organizations Mairead has cofounded, the Community of Peace People, organizes summer camps for young Catholics and Protestants from Northern Ireland. In her life's work to promote justice and peace by nonviolent means, she has visited more than twenty-five countries and met with world leaders including Queen Elizabeth II, Pope John Paul II, and President Jimmy Carter.

Not necessarily a predictable course from its beginning at a secretary's desk. But the course of one who responded to circumstances with courage, talent, and a belief in possibilities.

And there's Elisa, as fine an editor as ever lived, combining both the gentle touch required for handling writers—all of us temperamental and touchy—with a keen eye for whole pages of words that need nothing less than hacksawing. Perhaps this is because she's a writer herself. When Elisa had her first child, I received an e-mail from a mutual friend in publishing. "You may not have heard," he let me know, "that her baby was born with Down syndrome."

Resigning from her full-time editorial post, Elisa began doing freelance edit-
ing and writing from home to be more available for her daughter, who would
undergo open-heart surgery at six months. And in order to better care for Eden,
Elisa went back to school to become a certified nursing assistant.

"I've never been interested in anything medical-related," she says, "and suddenly I'm wearing scrubs and taking vital signs! Driving home from class, I found
myself thinking, *How did I get here?* But I believe this will somehow become a part
of my vocation."

There's such a complete absence of self-pity there and in what I've read of her
beautiful musings on watching her baby develop. There is also a delicate, difficult
balance between accepting that we're not ever in full control of our lives, yet refusing to be passive as we ask, *What can I learn from this? How can I respond faithfully
to this new season of life? How is God preparing me for what's up ahead?*

Any of us can go through seasons when some tsunami of the unexpected rocks
the plans we so carefully made. Suddenly the sky tilts, and every cloud in it and
every piece of our landscape has to adjust. We've lost our bearings entirely, and
only the days move us forward. But the remarkable thing is that those days do
bring healing and hope, and the future does begin to appear again—perhaps even
clearer than before the sea change we never saw coming.

Just Go

Gloria White-Hammond could not have mapped her path from beginning to end
even if she had tried. She loved her job as a pediatrician but found she couldn't
always assist at-risk kids, as she longed to do. She'd been serving in an urban medical clinic targeting low-income families, and her frustration in seeing those
patients for only a limited time helped create another avenue for helping these
families—and, in the process, helped clarify her own calling as a minister:

> In my medical practice, I was seeing so many girls who seemed to be lost,
> and I was feeling like I wasn't able to do enough.... So, I looked for another
> venue to connect with them.
>
> It wasn't necessarily starting out with a plan that said, "In January of 1994,

you'll start a girls' group." It wasn't like I planned to do it other than seeing a need and trying to get a sense from God of how to respond to the need.

I was interested in writing as a way of expressing my feelings and thought we might offer this as a tool for the girls. One of the members in our congregation was a professional writer, so I sold the idea to her. Our initial plan was to meet on a weekly basis.… But it became apparent that we would need to be even more involved in their lives, in a much more comprehensive way.

Thus was born Do the Write Thing. The girls involved, ages eight to seventeen, do much more now than write. Today the program has a full-time director in addition to drama, tutoring, and a host of other programs, including taking the girls to plays and introducing them to the work of African American women writers—giving them a vision for how they themselves might chart a new course.

"A lot of working with these girls," she adds, "is just hanging in through all their changes…which is of course what God does for us: waits until we get it, and keeps hanging in with us through it all. Which is the definition of grace."

Gloria has one answer, and only one, to how a child like her—often the only African American kid in an all-white army-base setting, the only girl without a date to the prom—grew up to be the woman she is, with all the richness, beauty, and craziness of her life:

I don't hear God perfectly, but I have learned over the years how to discern God's voice. I continue to learn how to just go ahead and do it: just go. It kind of gets down to that, having this very clear sense of calling, rising above my own inhibitions, which are many, and by the power of the Spirit go on out there.…

One of the things I've learned along the way is to say yes and trust as time goes by that God will let you know what you need to know. There have been some things God has said, and they've come to pass [right away], and then there have been other things that have been works in progress, things that have taken ten, twenty years for the evidence to be manifest. As I get older, I learn more how to be patient with the process and trust God, because I don't know anything else to do.

And, as if her career needed another even slight shift in its course, she's served as the national chair for the Million Voices for Dafur campaign to end genocide in the Darfur region of the Sudan.

In her personal life, she helps care for her husband's mother, who is in the middle stages of Alzheimer's and lives with them.

"How do we manage?" She laughs. "Well, first of all, Ray and I do it together, and that makes a huge difference. I do a lot of praying, and that's the other thing that makes a huge difference."

A woman of enormous courage is how I think of her and how the press describes her. She describes herself, though, as suffering from a "disease to please"—as pathologically shy.

And so I recall that actress Dorothy Bernard said, "Courage is fear that has said its prayers." Which is good news for those blessed among us who are born meek. And good news, too, for those who long for intricate maps for the journey ahead and get only nudges or tugs or a compass needle pointing only in a general direction.

It's all any of us can ask, and it turns out to be all we need: Being alert to our gifts and the needs around us. Seeking how God calls us to respond to those needs with our gifts. Listening. Waiting. And then, with a power beyond our own, learning to *just go.*

Loving the Big Wind

Learning to Live with Peace When It's Never Calm

F air winds and following seas" was how an old boyfriend signed his letters when
he wrote from the Merchant Marine Academy in Kings Point, New York.

It's been well over two decades since I gave away the stuffed animals this guy
won me at Six Flags and tossed all the old letters, but the one thing I've held on to
is the phrase: "fair winds and following seas." I like that. I like the sound of it and
the sentiment, speaking as it does of calm, nothing tumultuous or unexpected or
wild.

Though it has nothing to do with my life.

I once had a neighbor who was something of a sage. Not exactly the kind you
climb the Himalayas to sit cross-legged to meet. She was more the L.L.Bean type
of guru. This neighbor was a smart woman by any measure, but it was her throw-
away lines that always caught me off guard.

One spring afternoon I'd just completed my costume change from a business
suit—what I wear in my life as the mild-mannered English professor—into Super-
mommy wear: jeans and sneakers. The standard-issue superhero's cape is, of
course, part of the ensemble, though not visible to the naked eye. I was busy
retying my children's shoes and repumping their tires, but my mind was on a book
deadline galloping across the calendar toward me—I'm sure it moved itself up
when I wasn't looking. I also had a Mount St. Helens of exams to grade on my

desk. Between bike-tire pumps, I was berating myself out loud for trying to take on too much. What was the point of the stress? Why didn't I just quit teaching and quit staying up late to write by computer light?

"*Why* do I live like this?" I wanted to know.

"Because you like it," my neighbor said.

Just like that.

No particular value judgment of me. Or of herself. Good for her.

I shook my head as I felt for the tire nozzle cap. "Not today, I don't."

"Okay, maybe not today, but in general you *like* living like this. You choose this. And maybe you're thinking that you're *supposed* to want things calm and simple just adds to your stress."

I let my kids roll out in hot pursuit of her kids, and I mulled this over.

It was true.

This was how we lived: never sitting at anchor. We typically moved at a pace that was exhilarating. We'd already learned some hard lessons on knowing when to slow down, and how, and we'd soon discover we had more to learn.

But my neighbor was right. We had to pay bills, sure—that'll keep you setting the alarm. But it was more than that for my husband and me. This is what we thrived on. And my thinking that the lack of calm meant there was something wrong with our family only added to my feeling of not-calm.

For one thing, we seem to like to add another child to the family while in the midst of moving, and when moving, the relocation must be at least a thousand miles away. And if you've never moved with young children, you've never experienced the full relocation pathology: packing boxes—with little hands busily unpacking—and trying to guess how long you'll be in temporary rental housing and wondering if the boxes sent to storage will be stuck in some warehouse's Siberian nether regions until the baby will be driving.

Up until recently, we also regularly made our lives more complicated by rescuing another soon-to-be-perishing canine, feline, or equine—wait, that would be *I* have rescued too many four-legged creatures. The retired racehorse, for example, added little in the way of calm to our lives—including, we later discovered, greeting innocent, unsuspecting dinner guests just outside the front door: a thousand-pound butler who clearly needed restraining.

My neighborhood sage was right. Underneath layers of looniness and rush and clutter is a rich and full and challenging life. And it's this very sense of the good pulling against the good that reminds me it is a privilege to live in the midst of a tension I've chosen. And *cherish.*

Jesus Isn't Safe

I grew up in East Tennessee—that gorgeous, mountainous, moonshine-still-studded part of the state. In East Tennessee, we were raised to think of West Tennesseans as a staggering, neon-lit Beale Street kind of people who believe barbecue is made with beef instead of what the angels and all thinking people know to be right: pork. Middle Tennessee, we learned, was full of nothing but Nashville, that overgrown honky-tonk town.

As an adult who has lived all over, I've somehow looped back to God's own country, the Volunteer State, and have called that overgrown honky-tonk town home now for more than two years. And Music City is splendid, bursting with artistic energy. I like to pretend I'm the kind of person who is counting the days until our new world-class symphony hall is finished downtown, but the truth is I'm the kind of person who knows where Faith Hill lives—just down the street and, okay, around a few more—and the kind who drops little mentions to family and friends like, *At last Friday's Belmont basketball game, Vince Gill and I found the ref's calls to be pretty lousy. (Those of us who've seen him frequently and have almost met him call him Vince.)*

There is also a good deal of what's called contemporary Christian music in this town. On one particular Christian rock station, the music is marvelous, mostly, but the station's motto makes me want to put my fist through my dash: "Safe for the whole family."

Now I'm the mother of small children, and I understand that it's a good thing to have stations I can flip on without worrying about what new vocabulary my kindergarten boy will add to his already interesting list of Just Overheard. "Safe" can be comforting. But it's not what I've seen of Jesus. Jesus is the guy who tells people to step barefooted out on top of the water, whose followers live in caves, who asks fully employed people to leave steady jobs, who doesn't end life poolside with a full pension plan. Last time I checked, taking Jesus seriously is as dangerous a thing as a person could do.

Jesus is the place to come if you're looking for peace. But not for safety in the middle-class American sense. And not for calm.

One of the challenges of balancing family and career is to sort out the risk and adrenaline rush of following God out of the boat from the turmoil we make ourselves, a chaos that can disrupt and destroy. The chaos we create ourselves can look benign enough: a willingness, even eagerness, for change. A dissatisfaction with things as they are. But I've had to learn in my own life that these things can also be driven by mere restlessness or a longing to ignore the hurts of our lives.

The critic John Forster once said that Charles Dickens's characters were actually quite flat and only appeared to be real and three-dimensional because they vibrated so fast. I wonder if many of us haven't lived in that land at some time. But I've learned, and am still learning, that peace can exist in a life of crazy-paced days if purpose lives at the center. And I'm learning that safety can't be the primary goal if our purpose is following Jesus.

Untidy Lives

A friend from graduate school, Julia Lisella, was among the first of our cluster of doctoral students in English to venture into the uncharted region of motherhood, where no one, it was rumored, was giving out extra academic degrees for breastfeeding.

When Julia returned to work after her maternity leave, I wanted to know right away: "Well? How is it? Are you managing to get everything done?" She turned on me. "*Look* at me," she demanded. "*Look at me!*"

I did. Dark, Italian good looks. She could have been my husband's sister. "You've lost all your weight," I offered tentatively. "Good for you."

She shook her head impatiently. Only one earring dangled from one ear lobe, I noticed. The other was missing.

"And my hair," she insisted, "does it look like it's been fixed? Because it *hasn't*. For *weeks*."

"Well, but your hair always looks ni—"

"And do you have any *idea* how many hours they can make you sit in a pediatrician's waiting room? *Any idea?*"

I'd just been suspecting I was pregnant myself, and this was not the working-mommy public-relations shtick I'd been hoping to hear.

Julia and I have kept in touch loosely over the years, through finishing our degrees, through the addition of children, through her husband's going back to graduate school, through my too many moves, through various jobs on all sides. I heard from her again a few weeks ago. She is still teaching at Harvard, still writing poetry, still raising her kids. And life, she said, is crazy. Just crazy. And very good.

There can be something lovely, you know, about untidy lives.

A university administrator once called us from his cell phone to finalize a job offer for my husband. There's nothing extraordinary about such a phone call, except that the administrator was at that moment driving through a Wendy's pickup window with two of his three children in the back of the car, both of them trying to order at once. The kids had the day off from school, and the administrator had more flexibility in his work schedule that day than his wife. So here they all were, and the phone call was still getting made—if a bit interrupted by requests for more ketchup. Todd and I were in our car, going to the class I was teaching, and we could hear the chatter in the background and picture the scene: no doubt a few fries spilled on the seats. Far from being a sign to us of the man's lack of professionalism, the Wendy's call made us suspect that this would be a family of kindred spirits—and we were right. Husband and wife have become invaluable friends.

Untidy lives can be the sign of a lot going on—goodness and richness and purpose—under the surface. A surface that might be just a bit sticky and stained.

I remember the time I was asked, along with a couple of other women, to speak to a gathering of bright, professionally ambitious female undergraduates. We speakers were a broadcast journalist, a minister, and a professor—a kind of modern-day butcher and baker and candlestick maker. We'd been invited to speak because, the club's president announced, we were shining examples of having "successfully balanced career and family life."

God bless their sweet undergraduate hearts, but they had no idea.

We the speakers exchanged amused glances. I was wearing my Don't Mess with

Texas—or Me navy power suit which, I was just noticing, was not only badly rumpled but also covered in golden retriever hair. Not to mention the cuffs caked in mustard from my children's dinner. Oh, and there was a tiny hand print of, perhaps, chocolate. Taking clothes to the dry cleaners is one of those errands that drops down a laundry chute in my brain into nowhere and never gets done. The notes I would speak from had been scrawled at stoplights and stuffed in my pockets.

When it was my turn to speak, I stood behind the podium and realized the yellow remnants of my kids' dinner could probably be seen by at least the front fifteen tables. "If we are your models for success," I told the group, flaking mustard from my cuff, "you are in very big trouble."

Announcing that I came bearing good news and bad news, I gave them the bad news first: this balance of personal and professional life would almost assuredly be harder than they could ever dream. But here was the good news: it also just might be far more fulfilling, far richer, far more meaningful than they could ever imagine. While there was no one formula they could learn for "successfully" balancing all that they wanted to do, that was actually good news, too. They could make entirely different decisions regarding career and family from the women seated beside them and still applaud one another. They could be creative with how to use their professional skills. They could—and should—shift and rearrange how the personal and professional fit together at each new season of life.

In fact, even as I'm learning myself to shift tacks from season to season, I'm also learning to spot new friends by looking for condiment smudges or significant dog hair on some item of clothing they're wearing. A run in the pantyhose will also do—if it runs at least ankle to hem—and so will a price tag left hanging from the back of the neck like Minnie Pearl. For male friends, nonmatching socks will suffice. For mothers, a purse full of things that do not belong in a purse. Like a pair of a child's smelly socks. Or a great novel that's far too big for the bag. Or a utilities bill that should have been mailed three days ago.

During the final edits for this book, I was scratching away at the hard-copy manuscript and discovered two pages missing. Mistaken for scratch paper, one had been made into a paper airplane by my son and the other into a fabulous colored-pencil rendition of a great white shark by my older daughter for her brother. Ah, the dignity of my professional life. My husband snapped a picture of us holding the pages and laughing. And it strikes me that this may well be symbolic of life in this season: Welcome to Our World—Please Secure All Personal Items While Boat Is in Motion.

Documented Nuttiness

Sometimes the craziness of our professional and personal lives gets displayed in black and white. And it's not always pretty.

Not long after my husband accepted, with my support, the job from the nice man in the Wendy's drive-through, it was made clear to me just how nuts my life really was, thanks to a husband whose energy knows no bounds, thanks to three incredible kids, thanks to two sets of professional callings, thanks to our moving an average of every two years...*nuts*. Made abundantly, humiliatingly clear by the Texas Department of Transportation (DOT). My tax dollars at work.

As a rule, Texans are an unfailingly friendly race of people—and they do think they're their own race. They're loud and garrulous and generous in a ten-gallon hat, here-borrow-my-horse kind of way.

At the DOT, though, I found the *one* citizen in the entire Lone Star State who wasn't friendly—and this one could freeze-dry a stranger with a stare.

I had with me a good portion of the paper proof of my life up to age thirty-nine, with all the various metamorphoses nearly four decades had seen: A Social Security card with my maiden name, Joyce Lynn Jordan, issued in Washington, DC. A marriage license on which a clerk in East Tennessee, where we were married, made two words from one out of our new county of residence so that it announced to the world we'd be living in Middle Sex, Massachusetts. Given that she also misspelled my name, as Joy Jord*on*, I suppose we were also not quite legally married and were living in sin—in Middle Sex. I also had with me a passport for Joyce Lyn Jordan Lake, with the *n* dropped from the middle name and my married surname added. This was procured on a cold, rainy day in Boston from a Make My Day crabby kind of clerk—nobody does double-barreled crabby better than Bostonians in winter. Beside that was a recent pay stub from the university where I then taught. "Pay to the order of Joy Jordan-Lake," the stub announced—yet another incarnation.

"Well," I beamed at the DOT clerk, "my name sort of...evolved...you know how that goes."

She looked at me. She did not, apparently, know how that goes.

"I was born Joyce, but everyone always called me Joy, until one point in my early working days when I decided Joy sounded too, you know, kind of ditzy and blonde, like..."

She peered over her bifocals at me with a look that said *that* was precisely what she saw standing before her.

"And the last name," I tried, "for professional reasons..."

My last name morphed years ago into including a hyphen, partly because I'd wanted to keep some semblance of the name I'd started my working life under and partly because Joy Lake sounds—let's be honest here—like an amusement park way past its prime. Unless you're a masseuse or in the market for an alias in a witness protection program, Joy Lake really doesn't work so well as a professional name—or for that matter a personal one. But I didn't want an entirely different last name from my children, either. Which is how I became attached to the floating piece of punctuation.

"She has six names," the DOT clerk barked into a telephone, not even attempting to whisper. Then she narrowed her eyes at me. "What was the number of this alleged North Carolina license you lost?"

I tried chummy confidentiality: "Well, now, if I *had* it, I could tell you." Are there really people in the world who write down their license numbers in a separate, nonwallet place? Certainly no writers do. Okay, so my father would. But in the fifteen years since finishing Graduate Degree Number One, when normal grown-up people begin their journey from concrete-block bookshelves to mahogany organization, dependability, and stability, I'd moved another eight times, all over the country, and worked many jobs and bore a couple of children and dreamt of a third. I'd no idea where my obscure personal information was— or even what time zone it might be in.

"You *don't exist* in North Carolina," the DOT informed me. "There are no Jordans with this Social Security number in North Carolina."

"Ah, yes, but you see I was married at the time. In North Carolina. I would've been Lake. Or," I cleared my throat, "or maybe Jordan-Lake."

"You don't know who you are?"

"Well, *of course* I know who I am. See, I use one name professionally, but for my personal life—you know, like dinner reservations—I'm not so particular and…which would you say a driver's license would be?" I tried smiling winsomely.

The DOT spoke into the phone: "She's changing her mind, *again*, about who she is."

"No, see…I *know* who I am. It's just that I'm a writer, and my early bylines, back when I was a reporter, back before kids and—"

"She says now there's a *hyphen*," the DOT hissed into the line.

She set me sprawling on the pins of her two eye points. "I always tell people: don't use hyphens. You won't know who you are."

I could see she thought me one of those working women who is succeeding at neither—the work or the womanhood. But I'd show her. I leaned down to pat my son's curly head. Clearly a sweet, well-mannered child. Surely that showed I was a responsible *mother*, at least. If not a responsible person. After all, here I was, a working mother, here with one of my children, during the workday. Quality time: just him and me and the Texas Department of Transportation.

Justin smiled up at me. His face was clean. I looked to be sure that the DOT was noticing *my* child's cleanliness-next-to-godliness. She was, in fact, looking down at him—stonily. At three, Justin had blond, Shirley Temple ringlets and blue eyes. People *always* smiled at him. Strong men melted in his presence. What was *wrong* with this woman? I looked back at my cherub. He was holding his gum suspended in a lopsided, oval halo that ran from his mouth up over his curls and was just then being lowered to the back of his neck.

I pulled gum from the ringlets—at least one curl would have to be cut out—as the DOT snipped into me again. "Well, well. Here you are after all. In North Carolina. Expiration date?"

Ha! I had her there. I might be still mourning the surrender of my Massachusetts license, and I might have just lost my North Carolina license, and I might be not entirely legal to drive in Texas yet, but I knew my North Carolina license expired on my fortieth birthday, and *that* I *knew* had not yet come. One keeps track of these things.

The DOT ignored me as I pronounced the date, and she barked into the phone, "And when does she expire?"

Then she met my eye. "You'll be 'Lake' in Texas. Without any *hyphen*."

"Well," I said bravely, assertively, standing up for my womanly rights. Just like I'd learned in New England. And then added, "Okay." Because this was not New England but Texas, where people carried guns on their key rings. She was clearly a hiccup away from calling the state troopers.

Which she had to do anyway, as it turned out. "Car registration?"

"Well, *of course* I have the insurance information, you'll see here. In *Texas*," I added triumphantly. She was unmoved.

"Registration?"

"Yes, well, over the phone they said that with the insurance card someone could check my tag numbers. My husband is on a business trip, and my registration always stays in my glove compartment, you know, where we all put it, but he must have moved it—can you imagine?—and since I can't reach him…"

She called the state troopers.

When they gave her the information, she seemed incredulous that my car had been involved in no felonies, illegal border crossings, or bank heists. So far.

At last she took my picture for the official, laminated license and handed me a temporary paper certifying my Texas status.

"Here," was her benediction.

"Sorry I took so much of your time," I said.

She raised one eyebrow and lowered her ice-pick eyes to my son. I knew she was guessing that I didn't know who the father was.

In fact, en route home, it was the father himself who called from the trip he was on.

"Oh," he said sunnily. "Thought I'd returned that registration to your glove compartment. Oops."

His unshakeable cheerfulness can be truly annoying some days.

"Oops is right, Big Boy. And there was a little problem with my name."

"Your name?"

"Several of them. Different jobs and marriage and moves and…life seasons, you know."

"So you just explained. Right?"

Did I explain? Besides saying I was a writer, which hadn't seemed to help my sanity plea? I considered marching back in to the DOT to explain. That yes, indeed, my life was nuts—just like my name, just like the kaleidoscope of differ-ent jobs I'd held and houses my husband and I had packed and unpacked, just like those magnificent kids who kept our brains and our kitchen floor cluttered.

But my sails were full—and can't something be said for that?

And maybe there are a lot of me out there—like, perhaps…you?

I thought of Julia the poet with her single earring and disheveled dark hair.

And the boss who became a close friend after calling from the Wendy's drive-through window.

And my navy power suit cuffs so classily laced in kids' mustard.

I pulled more gum from my son's ringlets and laughed. Because sometimes, when we're paying attention, even the tension on our time can be precious, a sign that there is much, much blessing in the mess of our kitchen counters and lives. A sign that sometimes God fills our cup up with the blessings of family and work, both of which matter to God, and the cup runneth over and spilleth out onto the floor.

I wanted to tell the DOT that.

Peace, now *that* we can't live without.

But calm? Well…

Okay, maybe it's crazy some days.

But maybe—at least according to one neighborhood guru—maybe I, and maybe you too, maybe lots of us like it that way.

Avoiding the Shallows

Creating a Family Culture of Compassion and Service

T hree words caught my eye on the computer screen as I passed—an e-mail from a woman I'd just interviewed:

WE GOT THEM!

That was enough to yank me back to the desk.

I was in the midst of Real Life at my house, trying to herd small people toward bed so my husband and I could catch up on each other's days and so I could grade papers. But those three words halted my path through the house and made me stop to read the whole message:

> It is with unsurpassed joy and a significant amount of exhaustion that I can report to you, WE GOT THEM! Oh, just typing that...caused tears to roll down my cheeks. We experienced setback after setback.... This rescue was miraculous as all the news reports on what occurred still ponder how it was possible. This is a government that has had significant pressure to crack down from all over the world and never does anything. Then this small nongovernmental organization rolls into town with eleven employees, and three weeks later thirty-seven precious girls are in a place of safety. God is good and loves these gorgeous girls immensely.

Distracted and clumsy, I stumbled upstairs to tuck the kids in bed and have prayers. Together we thanked God for the good news in the e-mail.

My kids understood enough to at least pretend to be thankful with me: little girls on the other side of the globe were being badly mistreated, and a woman Mommy was interviewing for an article was involved with their rescue.

They didn't need to know the title of the article that was bumping around in my brain: "Pleasure and Profit: Children for Sale." Neither did they need to know the details. The woman I'd interviewed, Shannon Sedgwick (now Shannon Sedgwick Davis), worked at that time for International Justice Mission, an organization of attorneys and investigators that uses individual countries' own legal systems to document and help combat oppression, including forced prostitution, bonded child slavery, illegal detention and torture, sexual abuse, and widows' land-rights cases. My kids didn't need the details of how this woman had seen hell up close: little girls beaten, cigarettes extinguished on barely-past-baby skin, children as young as five sold day after day—and up to ten times a day—for the sexual pleasure of primarily Western men. They didn't need to know that the process of "purchasing"—raping—children in Svay Pak, a brothel-infested neighborhood of Cambodia, is as simple as buying a bag of rice—or perhaps easier.

My kids only needed to know enough to be reminded that their troubles that day—and mine—might have hurt us or angered us or saddened us for how we'd hurt others, but they probably didn't amount to much compared to the troubles of hurting little girls in Southeast Asia.

It's the kind of thing my kids need to hear, and I need to hear even more. To keep our very full lives in a larger perspective.

It's Not About Adding on Stress

To be involved in hands-on service and continually aware of the hungry and hurting of the world risks piling pressure on top of pressure for over-the-top, busy families.

"Are you sure you want to include this as part of the book?" one woman asked me. "We're already so stressed with our jobs and our kids. Do we need to feel even more guilty about one more thing we're not doing?"

A fair and good question.

Except that it's not about loading on guilt or adding to stress.

Maybe I should make some things clear. By nature, I tend toward worry and stress like a flower tends toward sun. But here's the odd thing: the best cure in any given day for lowering my own stress level and misplaced feelings of guilt is to compare my frustrations to anyone I know living and working in much more challenging conditions. I think of Shannon's words about attempting to comfort the nine youngest girls rescued from the brothel—the ones she calls "the babies":

> When I got there they were all on a cement bench, screaming and crying
> horrifically. I threw my backpack down and tried to put them all in my
> arms. We arranged to put them in a room where I continued to kiss them
> and hold them and wipe away their tears. Eventually they calmed down,
> and by the time we transported them to Bravo (the safe house), they were
> singing "Baby Shark" and "Peanut Butter Jelly" with me. Now there are
> nine Vietnamese children whose entire English vocabulary is "Baby shark,
> duh, duh, duh" and "Peanut butter, peanut butter and jelly." And "Shan-
> non," of course. I could not be more honored.

I've found that my own family just plain functions better when connected with what I have to remind myself daily are *real* problems: Not knowing how you will feed your baby even one more meal. Not knowing how your little girl will ever learn to read, since the schools where you live cost money, and you have none. Not having access, *ever*, to clean water. Not being able to afford even the most basic hospital care so that your elderly mother can die without pain.

My kids probably bicker and pick at one another at the usual red-blooded American rate—*except* when they're working for some greater good. Sorting clothes on a Saturday morning for a local shelter will bounce them back into line in a hurry. So will setting the tables on a Monday evening for Room at the Inn, a ministry for homeless men. Ditto for hauling mulch outside a transitional house for former drug addicts or loading groceries for Christmas-box deliveries.

If only out of self-interest in expanding the no-combat zone, we have to keep our kids, and ourselves, connected to worlds bigger than our own house. Sure, on most days our bookshelves and banisters may not pass a white-glove test. But in the light of larger concerns, who really cares? Okay, so there are those who care— and they can bring their own Endust when they drop by for dinner.

Involving the Whole Crew in Service

Now working for charitable-giving foundation Geneva Global, Shannon traces her own professional passions to how she was raised:

> My family was incredible at empowering me and encouraging me to be all I could.… They also involved me in tons of service projects ranging from mission trips to Mexico to being a camp counselor at a handicapped children's camp. They encouraged me to learn sign language and attain other [skills] that would uniquely equip me to serve. They also set a large example by way of their own lives. My parents have always served as long as I can remember, and we were always serving together as a family.

Connections with a wider and less privileged world don't have to be incredibly time-consuming. It can be life changing to spend family vacation time helping build cribs for an orphanage or homes in a region devastated by natural disaster. Our friends Jason and Elizabeth Rogers, for instance, will spend their three kids' upcoming spring break working in East Tennessee for Appalachian Outreach, where they might rebuild collapsed flooring in somebody's house or help patch a roof.

But lots of us still have children too young to be of much help in construction, or we can't arrange the time off when we're needed.

Many humanitarian aid agencies offer child sponsorships: World Vision, for example, and Compassion International. Or consider the Shalom Foundation, directed by Jacqueline Swartz, who left an established marketing job and sold her house in order to serve Guatemalan children in poverty. Or Sweet Sleep, founded by Jen Gash, who left a powerful position in a political official's office to help Moldovan orphans. Seeing a specific child's picture hanging on the fridge and knowing of his or her specific circumstances has a powerful impact on our own kids whenever they race into the kitchen, breathless, to tattle on the one who won't share the basketball.

And, not for the faint of heart, there is foster care. My kids' godparents, who excel in dealing with teens, have taken in a number of adolescents whose parents are in jail or who have been removed from their homes. And my hat's off—way off—to them. Or there's the model set by Pat Wilson, a law professor, and her husband, Mike Jones, the director of environmental services for his city. They're busy people with two biological kids and lots of church and civic leadership responsibilities. Mike and Pat have every reason, as far as I'm concerned, to hang the We Gave at the Office sign on their front door. Instead, they take in foster children. They've requested in particular biracial kids in sibling groups, the tough ones to place. And they nurture and guide and redirect these little ones, sometimes for years, until the glove-fit family comes along.

Now you can't take on extra lives in your house without making things more hectic. In fact, I've never heard Pat or Mike claim their lives are calm. Or quiet. But I do have to wonder if the depth and stability in their older kids stems from watching their parents take on more of what *and who* matters.

I want my kids influenced by these people.

I want them to know people like Jimmy and Janet Dorrell, who run the Church Under the Bridge in Waco, Texas, which sits, as its name would strongly suggest to those paying attention, under a bridge—an I-35 overpass, as a matter of fact, thundering from Laredo in south Texas to Duluth, Minnesota. Asphalt and diesel fumes and the screech of truck brakes pass overhead where there ought to be rafters and chandeliers. "Our church structure is federally funded," Jimmy likes to quip.

The Dorrells introduced us to Kathy Dudley. Long concerned with racial reconciliation and urban poverty, Kathy opened a shelter in her own home for inner-city castaways. I want my kids to know her.

I want my kids to know some of the stories from my own past: the woman I met at the Salvation Army in Louisville, Kentucky, who was running from an abusive husband and smuggling two children out in the process. She had not a dime to her name. Yet, thinking that I, too, was homeless, she offered to sell her own plasma, then lend me the money so I could buy some form of identification and sell my own plasma. Then, she said, we could *both* get something to eat. And she would trust me, she added, to pay her back when I could.

Or Amatul, who frequented the food pantry my friends and I ran in Cambridge. She had six kids and no job and no husband but was working toward her nursing degree—which she finished at last. And she came back to thank us and to accept the *way-to-go!* hugs we were waiting to pile on her.

I want them to know about Robin Hanna, the founder of Signs of Love, a program designed to find, befriend, and educate deaf persons in developing nations. When I interviewed Robin a couple of years ago, she recalled the corporate job in California that she'd left. I later read aloud from the interview transcript over the dinner table:

> I remember thinking, *Okay, this is it. The career that I love, I've got it.* And I love the finer things of life.... [I would] hear stories of people doing work in developing nations. And I would think *I'll support that....* I never thought it would be me.... [But] once a person goes to the developing world and sees the stark reality of poverty that is so much in your face and then you go back to your comfortable suburban lifestyle, you cannot get that image out of your mind.... If we will learn to...face fear instead of [embracing] creature comforts, we'd realize that there is so much more of a world than we ever thought possible out there.

The day Robin decided to tell her boss she was going to resign and work in Honduras, he came into her office and offered her a promotion. When one of her colleagues got word that she'd turned down the offer, he informed her she'd just made the most foolish decision of her life.

> I told him, "Well, I guess that depends on your perspective...." To this day I've not regretted one bit of the decision I made. One person has the capabilities to influence the world in a way that you can never even dream, if you're just willing to leave what we think is important behind—and I would never, never turn back from what I'm doing. Even if I never again earn more than three hundred dollars a month, I would never change what I'm doing.

But for those of us not currently living on the edge in the developing world, life can easily become all about *us*. Even our generosity and self-sacrifice channels back toward our own children.

My husband and I both have lived and worked, separately and together, in less-than-luxurious surroundings. And at earlier seasons of life, both of us have worked day by day alongside people who had never been to a dentist, people who had no coats or hats or mittens for their children in a New England winter, people who rummaged through trash yesterday looking for food.

Currently, though, our life is incredibly comfortable in terms of where we live and move and have our coffee.

Which can be dangerous if we let it. Too much comfort can send any of us into the shallows, where we get stuck and can't see how to sail our way out. Too much comfort can convince us that our worries over money and scheduling and the dishwasher that just quit working today are somehow on a par with a much bigger picture of what really matters.

This is where community comes in, and listening. And this is how sometimes we help guide each other along in a foggy season of faith.

When Sacrifice Becomes Gift

A community of faith, in fact, became central to my own family's thinking about compassion and calling and what that might look like in permanent terms.

For years, Todd and I had talked about adopting a child. We'd discussed this long before the existence of our first biological baby, in fact. For years, I'd found myself in tears whenever anyone spoke or wrote of taking in a child who did not have a home. I could feel my heart being pulled string by string until it had become completely unraveled.

But it wasn't until I could see the Big 4-0 looming ahead that it dawned on me that for years this thing had felt like more than a tug—more like one of those Think About This images God sometimes lowers down in your life like the chandelier in the middle of *Phantom of the Opera*. You either acknowledge it's there and figure out what to do about it, or you spend the rest of your life having to stumble over it.

Yet here I was, approaching an age when diapers for many of my friends and colleagues were becoming a distant memory.

And we were already so busy with two kids and two jobs and a host of things we already weren't doing terribly well. Many weeks, I felt as if we'd been shot out of a cannon on Mondays, only to land on the weekend, wondering what just happened.

But.

I asked a few questions of adoptive parents and skimmed a couple of Internet adoption sites. At least I'd meant only to skim. I was drawn in. With no Internet access in my home at that time, I sat in the library of the university where I worked and wept, just sobbed—much to the bewilderment, no doubt, of the undergraduates around me dutifully downloading chemistry assignments.

Clearly, I was certifiably insane to think that we had room in our lives to take on *anything* extra, or that, surrounded by hosts of examples of better parenting than we'd so far achieved, we ought to take in a child.

But.

One of the sites had a verse from Philippians on its first page: "For it is God who works in you to will and to act according to his good purpose."[1]

God. Surely that was the engine behind this compulsion. But didn't God understand we were barely managing our time and lack thereof as it was? That we weren't yet the kinds of parents—or for that matter people—that we wanted to be? That the two kids we already had were exhibiting minor behavioral issues that surely needed more intentional parenting? And all that was on a good day.

I'd always worked through the early years of both biological children, but because ministry and writing and teaching had all offered tremendous flexibility, I had at many points worked far fewer hours and taken jobs with far less résumé dazzle than I might have without children. But now I wanted to move forward, not backward, in my career and to put in more hours, not fewer, now that the younger of the two kids would soon be going to school.

We'd just taken a family vacation and were astounded at how easy it was to make speedy pit stops. Everyone was potty trained and able to run off excess energy quickly and efficiently in a McDonald's PlayPlace or a Cracker Barrel sidewalk—dodging the unwary in rocking chairs.

But.

This chandelier had been lowered into the middle of the place that must be my heart, and I'd been tripping over it for years.

So together Todd and I explored adoption and began the paperwork, with

Todd taking on the greatest time burden—what I called *his* pregnancy. (Only, life not being entirely fair, without the varicose veins and stretch marks.)

But with the paperwork for the adoption nearly completed, we began to panic that perhaps we'd understood wrong. Perhaps what God expected of us was merely softened hearts and open wallets. Maybe God just wanted to break our hearts a little more over children around the world without homes in order to respond in tangible ways, not actually take in a child ourselves, exhausted and inept and unqualified as we were. Maybe that was it all along.

We talked with our kids.

They were decisive. And unanimous. Well *of course* we still ought to take in a child who needed a home.

There it was. And they never wavered.

The deadline was approaching for the final financial installment, a whopper, and following that would be an official referral, with a child's name and a face. We knew that after that, emotionally, there'd be no turning back.

My friend Kelly, who spends much of her personal and professional time insisting that a life of faith must be lived in community, had convinced us to join a small-group study that met in her home. It was made up of couples, all of us with young children, all of us with careers, whether full sails or in some sort of temporarily anchored state. Todd and I were still without any referral of a particular child. The call to adopt was still only that: an idea, a compulsion that we might or might not have gotten from God.

One night in August, we were honest with the small group about our confusion and complete lack of clarity and how painful that was. They listened intently and gently began to ask questions.

One group member, Kari, contributed one of my favorite queries. "I know that for us," she said, "with two kids and two jobs, we've reached our tilt. So have you reached your tilt?"

It was a good question, and put in such a way that a writer-type like me could latch on to the image and hold it.

She's right, of course. Every marriage has to know when it's at capacity. Perfectly good boats capsize for simply being too full and running too hard and too fast against the wind.

Todd and I were unanimous and decisive—in saying that we didn't know. Or maybe, yeah, we thought that we had reached our tilt. But if this was a calling, could it be that God would provide whatever of the extras—the time, the money, the increased parenting wisdom—that we needed? Or were we forgetting the way God not only gives the strength for what we need to do but also expects us to act like rational people at least vaguely aware of human limitations—like a need for sleep?

Then another friend in the group, Frank, offered this insight: "There is a little girl somewhere in China that perhaps you thought you would be adopting, but if you don't, and you know we'll all love you either way, I truly believe God has some-one in mind to love and to be a family for that little girl. God *will not* forsake that little girl. You need to know that."

We all fell silent.

We ended by praying together, as fervently and as honestly as I ever recall pray-ing in a group setting, and then went home. And I think most of the group assumed that we'd made our decision.

And, as it turned out, we had.

But not the one all of us left thinking we had.

Somehow Frank's insight was the arrow that hit home. Though he was offer-ing love and support for us to withdraw from the adoption if we needed to, he also brought forward the heart of the matter. I agree with him that God provides people for what needs doing in the world, and I'm not so self-deluded that I believe myself called to every place and every time and every hurt. In the past I've worked with urban homeless women and children, but I'm not there now. I've served soup to men with substance-abuse issues, but I'm not ladling now. My husband has dug latrines and wells in South America for villagers with no clean water and lobbied for more migrant farm-worker legislation in California. But he's not there now. And I do believe God is providing other people to fill those roles now. Other Not-Us people.

But there's a difference between a God-given calling and thinking one can be the answer to all the world's ills. The latter is a messianic complex and requires therapy—sometimes heavy sedation and straitjacketing. So it's the former I'm sug-gesting we might want to embrace.

Here was the thing: Frank was right. God *did* have plans to take care of that one little girl. And even in the midst of the pain and chaos of our lives just then, it became clear to both Todd and me that in this case, in this time, we were what God had planned for that little one—wacky and flawed and far, far from ideal as we were. So somehow God would have to help us push the limits of our tilt or give us wisdom for what to cut out in life, where to ditch the excess that could threaten to swamp our little boat.

And then, one fine blue-skyed day in October, three pictures appeared on my computer screen—photos sent from the Chinese Center of Adoption Affairs to our agency in the States, to my little office in Texas. The photos showed a big-eyed little girl, pale and thin, skin like white silk, four months old at the time of the picture, with a full head of thick black hair and an oval face that looked out at the world with terror and sorrow.

And from that moment, she was as much my child, as much heart of my heart, as either of the biological children I'd borne. It was as if I were looking at a third—or maybe fifth—trimester ultrasound in full color, with a baby who happened to be sitting up by herself outside my womb and waiting to feel a heartbeat next to her own.

There was no more noble intention from that moment, not another thought of the sacrifices we would have to make in order to bring her to us and make room for her in our lives. She was already a part of us, her presence already carving out space that willingly, eagerly, gave way. We were the privileged recipients of a treasure.

After many a family conference and with the help of Chinese friends, we'd already chosen the name Jasmine Li, the middle naming meaning "beautiful" in Mandarin—though depending on the intonation, also including "plum" and "strength."

On the day the pictures arrived on our screens, so did a brief description of Jasmine's background: she'd been found early one morning in January in the open-air market there in Yuan Jiang, Hunan, and had been wrapped in carpet with a small bottle tucked inside. Her cries had been heard by an older woman who worked in the market, an older woman who faithfully carried my daughter out of the biting winter cold and to the orphanage—an older woman named Li.

Months before we knew her story, we'd unknowingly named Jasmine after the woman who perhaps saved her life, a vital part of the chain that brought us together.

On the day that Jasmine's pictures appeared on my screen, my husband was out of town at a job interview a thousand miles away, and we could only talk and cry and celebrate together over the phone. He would have to ask permission of a secretary at the university where he was interviewing to print out his new daughter's picture for him—so he could then show it around to complete strangers who, as it turned out several months later, would become colleagues.

I was desperate to share my new daughter with someone. I looked at my calendar. Weeks before, I had scheduled lunch with my English department colleague and fellow church member, Brenda, who happened to be also the mother of two adoptive children. God gave me a friend in that moment who knew firsthand the miracle of this computer-screen birth, as real, as powerful as a birth of blood and water and too-bright lights.

When my aunt Joyce saw the pictures on her computer, she pronounced, "Why that child is cold and lonely." And in her good farm-girl, do-something-about-it way, she promptly made and mailed a soft pink and yellow rag quilt.

The three different photos showed Jasmine looking panic stricken and in pain—we learned later she'd probably had a perpetual ear infection since birth. In the three pictures, she wore three different outfits, bright polka-dotted, clashing monstrosities, but no doubt the best and the warmest the unheated orphanage had.

My feisty girlfriend Ginger, an endearing mixture of utterly unworldly compassion *and* a keen, even merciless fashion sense, called my cell phone that afternoon. Ginger, whose given name is Virginia Rose, was born in Alabama. I could hear the sweet tea and moon-on-magnolias behind every syllable, even though she was calling from her current home in New England.

"She is beautiful!" she shouted into the phone. "And I mean *beautiful!*"

We spent several loud moments agreeing on this together.

Then there was a pause. I knew what was coming.

And here it came: "But, girlfriend, what are we gonna *do* about that *wardrobe?*"

Only partially trusting my taste, she sent gifts.

Two months later, our new baby daughter slept with the pink and yellow rag quilt, as well as the hand-crocheted blanket my mother made her and the velvet-soft panda and the Chinese baby doll for which my mother-in-law scoured L.A.'s Chinatown.

Jasmine no longer looks cold. Or lonely. Or terror-stricken. The dimples on either side of her chin and the eyelashes nearly the length of her fingers and a three-steps-past-gregarious personality charm everyone in her path.

And, yes, Virginia Rose, there is a Santa Claus…bringing a torrent of gifts that December for Jasmine—meaning a wardrobe even you would approve.

Kids Making a Difference

Ten months later, at a rickety card-table stand in a blistering Labor Day weekend sun, my three kids sold twenty-dollar brownies. And the lemonade—who knows what that averaged a glass. Never much of a businesswoman myself (few writers are, which is why God created the sun and the moon and the literary agent and called it good), I couldn't bear to see how much cold, hard cash was being handed in big wads through car windows to the same little hands that have trouble keeping up with tooth-fairy quarters.

The older two kids, ten and six, had made a sign for Hurricane Katrina victims, while our toddler sat in her stroller and worked on her own contribution to curb appeal, which included smiling and waving. In large hand-markered, blue letters, the sign assured neighborhood drivers-by that 100 percent of all profits would go straight to New Orleans—presumably without passing through Toys "R" Us. I learned later that it was my older daughter, born with the ringmaster's flair for the dramatic, who'd coached her curly headed kindergartner brother to stand on the neighborhood median, feet carefully straddling petunias, and hold the sign, his cheeks sucked in, mouth turned down, and eyes unfocused to suggest, it would seem, the ravages of malnutrition and physical want. Or maybe it was to suggest the kind of pout into which he might fall if the passing car failed to stop. I didn't ask. My husband and I were too busy shoveling out brownies that, as a pan, were worth more than one of our cars.

Thanks to generous neighbors and to national media that was keeping us all apprised of the posthurricane tragedy, the kids made a bundle that weekend, and the cash did indeed find its way to where it was promised. The two older kids had chosen to miss their last day of swimming at the neighborhood pool for the season in order to run the stand—and I've never seen them so excited. Julia and Justin beamed as they scurried to fill orders. Meanwhile, baby Jasmine raised her hands over her head in Pentecostal delight and yelled, "Aaaaaaaaa!" which meant, in this context, "Thanks for sharing" and sometimes, "Hey, shouldn't someone who drives a Jag shell out a little more?" and, alternately, "Part of that brownie had better be coming to me."

I was already charbroiled myself, sweaty and tired, and might not have put up a fight if the kids had been ready to quit. But I kept my mouth shut and crammed more crisp green Lincolns and Jeffersons and Washingtons into the Quaker Oats box.

Lest I'm painting halos on little people who are—*well, what a coincidence*—related to me, lots of kids in lots of places were doing similar things that very same weekend in the wake of this natural disaster of epic proportions. All those kids knew something about what a good time looks like. They knew that sometimes the best of times comes from the hardest work—and not always work that leads to more Legos and the iPod that everyone else owns.

There's a certain *Yes!* shout to life when you actively make a difference, knowing you can contribute something of who you are and not just wait around for things to change. Kids learn this from us and from their teachers and coaches and mentors. They watch to see what gets us grownups jazzed, what makes us curse under our breath, what we're willing to run late for, what we're willing to ditch for something else.

Big Brother is indeed watching.

And so is Big Sister.

And Little Sister.

They're watching and deciding just what is important in life.

Now *that* would be pressure—and a lot of potential for learning the joy of making a difference.

What Heaven Looks Like

Here's what Shannon Sedgwick wrote from Southeast Asia just after the sting of the child prostitution ring. I read part of her letter to my kids:

> I worried that these girls were ruined and our work would go more to save the next generation rather than this one. But I was wrong. They are children still. They play and sing.... They crawl in my lap and kiss my cheeks.

They cry at night when we put them to bed. They have been damaged, but I believe there is significant hope for the younger ones for sure.

In the abused bodies of five-year-old girls, Shannon has seen horror. But she has a different take on it: "Nom, Lan, and thirty-five others are free.... It was the closest I have ever come to seeing my God as I played with their beautiful smiling faces. I can only imagine what heaven looks like, but I did get a glimpse—in Cambodia of all places. I am certain of that."

Like you, I'd love nothing more than to protect my three kids from every bad dream, every middle-school slight, every heartbreak ahead. Every fear of being abandoned—for the first time or again. Every moment of being disillusioned in human nature.

But I can't do that.

What I *can* do, however feebly, is try to lead them to a God who is with us, who works through us and beside and beyond us—who brings hope. Who *is* hope. Even when hope is nowhere else in sight.

Forever and Ever and...

I just put Jasmine down for sleep, mounded under her favorite blankets and quilt—but only after we've read her own Leaning Tower of Pisa of books. She likes ending with a sweet picture book in which a baby deer, baby duck, baby mouse, baby bear, baby owl, and baby person all ask, "Do you love me, Mama?" to which they are each told in various poetic ways, "Yes, little one, I love you as high as the...as strong as the...as long as the...forever and ever and always."

"Always!" Jasmine shouts, hands overhead, after each little creature is reassured.

"Always," I whisper back to her over and over again. "You are loved, Jasmine Li, forever and ever and always."

My home office shares a wall with the room where she's sleeping. As I settle back in with my laptop amongst crumpled notes and a Schlotzsky's iced tea and a half-eaten doughnut and a chapter to finish, I hear one more word from the bedroom, Jasmine's last call as she drifts off to sleep.

I stop tapping at keys to listen more closely.

"Always," she's saying.

Man–and Woman–Overboard

When the Marriage Capsizes

In a predominantly African American congregation where I worshiped sometimes while living near Monroe, North Carolina, one older man regularly
stood, and while the organ keened behind him, he'd say in a deep, time-graveled
baritone, "Lord, I just want to say thank you. Thank you, Lord, for this day."

That's right, we said back.

"Because Jesus, I know…"

Yes, Lord.

"I know that…"

Mm-hmm.

"You didn't have to wake me up this morning."

That's right.

"But you did. And I thank you."

No matter how many times I heard it, that profound gut-sense of gratitude
struck me, that way of living and moving that never takes mercy for granted, all
wrapped up in grace like the blanket you brought with you from bed.

But to be that grateful for a morning or a day, like it's a treasure and a surprise, you have to have been in a place where it wasn't a given. You have to know what it's like to be shipwrecked, bloodied, and sore, but somehow washed up on the sand instead of lost in the waters. *Gratitude. Mercy. Grace.* I know what these mean now.

Diving for a Mast

Many marriages go through a dark, stormy season, something more sinister than just the summer thundershowers that blow through as a natural part of two human beings' breathing, brewing coffee, and bolting for work from the same home base. Add to that the Wait-There's-More stress of deciding how to discipline children and pay mortgages and agree on who will spend four hours of his or her workday at the pediatrician's office, and there's plenty of potential for blue skies turning to clouds and clouds going heavy and black.

Sometimes, though, a marriage simply capsizes. Maybe it's been a long time in coming. The relationship has seen too many storms, and everyone is too exhausted to keep bailing out water. Sometimes one person gets too engrossed in something outside the marriage—the work that becomes all-consuming—and the whole boat pitches sideways. Sometimes the time pressures of kids and careers keep two people who once stayed up late trading grand ideas and big dreams now only rushing past each another, unspeaking except about schedules, just co-workers in a flight-control tower.

Back in my Head Sailing Instructor days at the Very Cool Camp in North Carolina, we spent one entire day teaching the boys to capsize their boats. On a sticky, breezeless July afternoon on a long wooden dock that stretches its arms like an embrace far out into Lake Eden, it takes very little nudging to send six- to thir-teen-year-old boys into the water.

Besides wearing out whole legions of overenergized, too-healthy boys as a favor to exhausted cabin counselors, the exercise was meant to teach my intrepid little sailors how to right a sailboat that capsized unintentionally. It was always one of my favorite days of sailing class: watching the white sails swoop in graceful arcs, then the splash and whoops of the swamped sailors, racing each other to scramble up on the daggerboard and leverage their trusty vessels upright. After I'd explained the technique—now that I'd learned it myself from the Boy Scout handbook—I issued the only real rule of the day: they must right their boats fairly quickly and not allow the hull to turn all the way upside down, to "turtle." This is when the mast could slide out of its hole in the hull, pull loose from the halyard and mainsheet, and drop to the soggy bottom of lovely Lake Eden. And someone would have to go diving for it.

But they were *boys*—the problem, in a word. And being boys, they wanted to push the exercise to its limit, to see how far, how fast, how fabulously close to disaster they could go. So inevitably, at least one adorable pair would feign incompetence and slip and flop and flail about their capsized hull like the Keystone Kops gone maritime. These were the boys who waited too long, who had to see what happened *if.* Or who just got sloppy, got lazy, didn't give a rip.

And someone would have to go down, go deep, feeling through mud for a mast.

Hurricane Season

When our hurricane season hit, it was nothing like the squalls that had become a part of the rhythm of our lives. Suddenly the shores all seemed to have dark, slippery sides with no handholds that I could find. We'd been seven years in laughing together, in working together, in being best friends. But in those seven years storms had been brewing, even on the sparkling June afternoons when we romped at Good Harbor Beach or the drizzling May mornings when we ate fresh-baked pastries on Helmut's deck in Rockport. Because even on the happy, glittering days, we were building bad habits. Criticisms like cannon fodder making craters in the earth. Angry ruts of the same arguments never fully resolved no matter how long we took to trace out each twist and turn of He Said, She Said, His Tone, Her Tone.

Neither of us ever abused the other. Yet somehow our marriage got battered. Somehow we were regularly doing damage to our friendship, our trust, our desire to stand side by side or to see the other's face over coffee. Plenty of marriages limp along, and no one ever hurls a chair or a plate, no one ever physically harms the other, no one verbally assaults the other, and yet both people walk away beaten.

When we finally noticed we were in trouble, the steady succession of earlier storms had worn us both out. Over and over and over, we'd capsized—I knew that—but for years we'd kept coming back up. We'd had so many laughs, so many beautiful moments on even the stormiest days, we hadn't noticed how exhausted we were from too many times of hauling sodden sails back up out of the water. Our lives together had turtled like the sailboats of all those summers ago, and by the time I noticed, I wasn't sure we had any energy left to survive.

Mommy, Daddy, Baby

Granted, we were both working too much and for the same church, we were both earning graduate degrees, we both had writing deadlines, and our only child at the time had become suddenly mobile. But even more challenging than the balance of parenting and career was the fact that we'd never learned how to deal well with the *very* different ways we approached conflict. The time pressures of kids and career didn't cause our troubles, but like any additional weight on an already weak structure, they merely revealed the fissures that were already there, the cracks and weak joints we'd both brought with us into the marriage.

It wasn't as if Todd and I didn't know the standard marital dangers. We'd been there as witnesses and counselors when other marriages hit nasty shoals. We knew the signs of trouble when we saw them sitting across the Formica-topped table from us. But in our own marriage, we didn't see—or maybe chose to ignore—them. We were, after all, mentors for other people. We had an image at stake: a less-nicely-sculpted Barbie and Ken in cheap tweed and sensible shoes. But now Barbie and Ken had taken on water and were going down.

Our daughter, just beginning to talk, began being honest about the state of things before we did. "Mommy sad," she reported to my parents on the phone.

We'd tried to hide the worst of the troubles from our daughter, but the tension stayed in the air like smoke, and there were my tears on her cheeks every night when I thought she'd drifted to sleep.

It was a Thursday, my morning to leave for work early, my husband's day to stay with Julia. I squatted down to hug and kiss her, long and hard, but hardly acknowledged my husband's attempt at "Good-bye. I love you."

That morning, there were no sharp words, just a quicksand silence, a void where there ought to have been some affection. A hole.

I had my keys in my hand and had reached the door.

My daughter leapt for the exit and blocked it with her little body.

"What is it, honey?" I was barely holding things together enough to speak any more.

She pawed at my hand holding the keys and tugged at the key ring. I opened my hand.

Encased in plastic and attached to the ring was a picture—of her in my arms and of my husband and me. All of us upstairs in my study. All of us standing close together and smiling.

"Mommy, Daddy, baby!" she pointed with a chubby finger to it and cried. *"Mommy, Daddy, baby!"*

These three go together, she was saying, and you big people are letting us fly all apart.

Nineteen months old. But she knew.

When friends and parishioners asked, in those dark days, how we were doing, not thinking they would hear anything back but what our culture says we can say—"FineHowAreYou"—I was honest. I had nothing left to be anything else. From their startled expressions I was vaguely aware I was crashing through rules.

"Not well," I would say. "Things are a bit rough. Thanks for asking, though. You?"

We'd performed the wedding ceremonies for more than a few of the couples in our church. What did that mean for them if our marriage couldn't survive?

It isn't true, you know, about our lightening each other's burdens. When we really care for each other, we U-Haul others' troubles on top of our own. My grief becomes their grief and theirs becomes mine. I could see this in their wide, frightened eyes. It was as if the ripping and tearing of Todd's and my life was ripping at threads in theirs, too.

"Want to do lunch?" some asked, looking scared.

"No. But thanks," I would say.

"Coffee?"

"I can't," I said. And I couldn't.

"May I come over and we can talk?"

"No."

"How 'bout if I call you?"

"No."

Their faces looked stricken.

"Maybe...," they said.

No no no no no.

Though sometimes I relented a little. "If you'd like to leave a message on the machine, that'd be nice," I'd tell some, to give them something to do. To help. They looked desperate; I could see that. By that time, I felt only numb.

"We"

Timing it so I'd get her voice mail, I called my editor for the book that was due in a few weeks. "I'll meet my deadline," I confessed to a tape, "but I just wanted you to know how things are. I don't want to talk about it, I can't, but in case I'm hard to reach by phone..."

I got an e-mail back that same day. "We prayed for you today," she said, "in our editorial meeting." There wasn't much more than that. And more wasn't needed.

Each Sunday, too, I saw concern on the faces around me. We'd married Julie and Vince the summer our daughter was born—three weeks, in fact, after the birth. Throughout my pregnancy, which was also their engagement, Vince had talked to my tummy weekly as he lobbied the still-swimming baby to hurry it up and arrive early so we could make the trip to perform the wedding. He'd carefully calculated the last possible day she could be born and still be old enough to make the eight-hour drive: July 12.

"But that's two weeks early," I'd laughed at him. "And first babies are most often late."

She was born July 12.

In an outdoor ceremony in a West Virginia state park, Todd and I had taken turns asking Julie and Vince to "Repeat after me."

Now nineteen months later, they were sitting side by side, husband and wife, just as we'd pronounced them by the power vested in us, and their eyes were full and they wanted to know, "Are you all right? You and Todd?" They weren't being polite. They really wanted to know.

I squeezed their hands. To take the place of what I couldn't say: *You can pray. Because I can't.*

Maybe they heard what I never said.

"We'll get you through this" was what kept coming back.

We. *We'll* get you through. Over and over and over, the We. We the editors. We your friends. We your family. We your parishioners. We who may have no clue how prayer really works but believe down to the bone that it matters. We're praying. We're standing here so you don't have to. We're holding on so you can collapse.

The wisest among them never said, "Everything's fine."

The wisest could see that it wasn't.

But the We kept rolling in, waves and waves on our dried-up shore. *We're holding on for you.*

Words Honestly Spoken

I found strength, too, in my memory of another marriage that crashed: the couple who had conducted our premarital counseling, Gloria and Ray.

Treating us to Boston's Legal Sea Foods for our final session of premarital counseling, they spoke of their own dark days in their marriage. Gloria, in particular, was brutally honest.

"We were going down," she said in a husky voice, "and I didn't care who we took with us."

Ray nodded but tried to soften the picture a bit. "Well, it was—"

"No," she stopped him. "We were going *down.*"

He toyed with his calamari. "Yeah," he said. "Okay."

"And didn't care *who* we took with us."

He thought a moment. "Yeah," he said. "Okay."

There was a little more detail maybe—but not much. Just the fact that things had hit some kind of rock or sand bar they hadn't seen coming, though they'd been on the approach for a long time.

I should've called them, of course, seven years after Ray spoke in our wedding sermon from Ecclesiastes of "a cord of three strands"[1] that would hold our marriage together. But I didn't. I couldn't speak.

And yet they spoke to me, seven years before by being brutally honest. *Going down,* they'd said, still visibly shaken as they remembered.

Those words seemed irrelevant to me at the time, my hand resting with its new diamond on the table. But the words lodged in my memory and stole out now to comfort me. Someone else had gone down thinking it might be for good, and they had come back up. And survived. And more than that, flourished.

Their long-ago words, only a thread of a much larger story I've never known, became a lifeline they'd tossed to us across the years.

Looking for Change

Todd and I saw a counselor together once and each separately once. And that was all. For anyone in that predicament asking my sage advice, I'd definitely recommend more. But I wasn't taking my own advice at that time.

The first counselor we saw together listened as we described our two in-process graduate degrees, our several jobs, our ministering in a church on the same staff, our different leadership styles, our different family backgrounds, our very different ways of expressing anger, of working things out…

"This," the counselor pronounced, "was a system just waiting to crash."

I've never been sure how helpful that was.

The second counselor I saw on my own: a thoroughly kind, empathetic man with soft hands and a still softer voice. He listened to me, then earnestly offered an insight or two—some of them helpful. Then he looked deep into my eyes to let me know this was what I'd come for today, this was the key: "You know, it's crucial to remember," he said, *"you can't change anyone."*

I thought about this. I thought about Todd. About me. Our daughter. Our future together.

"Watch me," I said, or something equally rude. I paid him. I put on my coat. I walked across the street and bought a ninety-cent bottle of fingernail polish, which I used only once (I'm not much on nails) right there in the car. I've no idea why this helped, but it did.

Or maybe it was the counselor saying, so kindly, so gently, what I so violently did not believe.

I drove home.

Told Todd about the session.

Saw him smile, wanly.

At least on that we agreed.

It might go against what graduate programs in counseling stress to their students, but at least we two agreed that the conventional knowledge for us was bunk. We would *both* have to ask for change from each other, or our marriage was not going to last.

During this time, I tried to write because there were deadlines to meet, but the sentences, when they came at all, were coming only in spurts. I tried to sleep but was too fitful. I rose early to exercise so I wouldn't punch holes in the world.

I tried to pray but was too angry. I could pray only that maybe someone else was praying.

At least some of my anger I aimed at God.

Todd came to faith during his college years at Harvard. And like many adults who can point to a clear before and after, his was a faith that emphasized *then* and *now*. My faith, on the other hand, had been one of progression. So I tended to speak of *journey* and *growth,* avoiding language that would exclude or offend or imply that someone else's journey might lead up paths I didn't approve of or couldn't pronounce. The before-and-after crowd, like Todd, could be touching from a safe distance, but up close, quite frankly, they made me nervous back then.

So when my frustration bubbled up to the surface and the earth's crust burst, I challenged my husband. "If Jesus makes such a difference in your life," I told him through clenched teeth, "then let's see the change." I probably slammed something down on the counter. And then I added, "Maybe change in me, too!" not because I really thought I was part of the problem, but because it sounded less arrogant. "If Jesus makes such a difference," I said, "let's see him change *us!*"

It wasn't a prayer at all or even a remotely religious moment. It wasn't an invitation for us to reconcile. I think I meant it as a parting shot.

"Yes," Todd said, not taking the bait, not defending himself. "You're right." I waited for the fight. "You're right," he said quietly. "You are absolutely right."

Which, maddeningly, is tough to keep swinging at.

Sharks Not Swimming; Italians Not Talking

Todd found that often when he began to explain or apologize, he ended up on the attack—or at least I perceived it that way and became only more incensed. So he decided at one point to make a Trappist monk of himself and quit talking altogether. As a spiritual discipline. As a way to save his marriage and his neck.

"My tongue gets me in trouble," he discerned, "so I won't use it. I'll write you notes, and that way I'll learn to think before I say something to you."

Well intentioned, certainly. I gave him credit for that.

But my husband is Italian. His father, of Canadian and Czech ancestry, died when Todd was young, so Todd was raised by his full-Italian mother and grew up with a loud, fun-loving, good-looking flock of Italian cousins. That was one of the reasons I'd married him—that quick, edgy wit, those stunning black curls and black eyes. I'd read *Wuthering Heights* many times from girlhood through graduate school and never before known anyone whose eyes could actually turn black when he was angry as Heathcliff's did. Until I met Todd.

So my husband, who is far more Italian than his watered-down genetic mix would indicate and whose eyes turn black when he's mad, began his vow of silence.

"I'm guessing I know," he scribbled to me in one of the early hours of the early days of his not speaking, "why not many Italians are Trappists."

It was pitiful, really. *He* was pitiful.

Sharks must keep swimming if they are to stay alive; Italians, I learned, must keep talking.

I watched my silent, still-gesturing husband's energies wilt, his vitality—of which there is so much—wither hour by hour.

I was intrigued.

And not in a terrible rush to stop it.

In the silence, I heard his humility. His commitment to change. Or to let Jesus do that, whatever it took.

In the silence, too, I began hearing some painful things about me. Not from Todd. Just in the silence. The whisper that speaks the whole, peeling, rotted, termite-ridden truth that we don't want to know about who we are and what we've done and what we're perfectly capable of doing.

The Doggedly Faithful

My friends Elizabeth and Pete informed me that I was coming for brunch, and they wouldn't take no for an answer. They'd been in the hospital waiting room for the birth of our first child, and Todd and I had been there for theirs. Been there, in fact, when the two of them first met. We'd been the ministers at their wedding ceremony. And at Pete's dad's funeral. We'd been there for each other at the crucial junctures, the detours and dead ends and back stretches of each other's professional and personal lives.

They'd earned the right to *tell* me I was coming to brunch.

And the doggedly faithful like them weren't few in number. They each had their ways of letting us know they were there—like so many hands linking themselves into a net we hadn't known was there when we first felt our grip slipping and the mast dropping down.

The friends who didn't flinch in the face of our storm became precious.

Years before, Todd and I had answered the phone in the charcoal hours of the almost-morning when another friend, Jan, called from the hospital to say her husband, Paul, had been hit by a car while riding his bike.

We'd been there when Jan came out of ICU, where she'd stood watch over Paul's body, being run now by machines and without much of a face.

"I held his hand," she'd told us, looking past us out the window. "And I told him," her voice snagged a little on tears she wouldn't let come, "that he was sexy."

Years before that, when I was first getting to know Paul, he made me nervous.

"How's your spirit?" he'd want to know.

I didn't say, "None of your business"—my southern mama had raised me better—but I thought it. Until I learned who he was and how much he meant what he said. He didn't want to hear *what* you were doing, just *how*—how you were doing on the inside.

We prayed in those days, all of us, when Paul couldn't. We showed up at their children's school plays, while Paul couldn't. Whole crews of us took turns trolleying their kids to lessons, while Paul couldn't, and Jan, caring for him, didn't have time.

Paul lived. The doctors pieced him together again little by little, returning the

explosion of laugh and the again handsome face—with a few scars to add interest—and the boisterous, gentle spirit we all loved.

But there had been dark nights that slid into dark months of no guarantee.

So when Jan touched my shoulder and said—did she say anything?—maybe
just looked hard in my eyes, I felt all those hospital weeks, all those months of horror and prayers and dry bones come alive. She looked hard in my eyes, always more
prone to spill over than hers, and she didn't have to tell me. I felt the net underneath me. Underneath us.

Which is why religious types make me so sad. I mean the types that when
they're in a church, act like they're in a church. Say nothing but what sounds
churchy. Never say one single true thing about who they are and where they're
struggling and where they're really blowing it.

And no one asking, "So how's your spirit today?"

Frightened by Each Other's Storms

I was once part of a Bible study full of good souls but typical of many church
groups in how we circled, tiptoeing, around the gritty issues of life. The group was
stocked like a trout pond with PhD's in religious issues: scriptural languages,
church history, theology, those kinds of things. These were bright minds and kind
hearts, better on both counts than my own. But one week I stuck my head up out
of the gopher hole to observe that, was it just me, or did we really seem to talk very
little of how our study applied to tough, private parts of our lives?

"For example," I said, looking around for the safest example in the room and
spotting Rob and Susan (not their real names). I'd just talked at length with them
the previous night, and I had been impressed with their professional and personal
lives, with their devotion to their biological kids and to a foster kid they'd taken in.
"For example, we wouldn't know if Rob and Susan's marriage was falling apart."
We all laughed at the preposterousness of the thought.

It wasn't spiritual discernment on my part so much as my tripping over the
truth on the way for a refill of coffee.

A few days later, Rob and Susan made an appointment with the group leader.
They wanted him to know they understood that I'd picked them as an example

precisely because I'd have assumed they were the safest of bets. I'd been clumsy, maybe, but not malicious—they understood that. And, they smiled grimly, the point I'd so clumsily made was a good one. Because their marriage was *indeed* falling apart, and nobody knew. But now, they both said, it was too late to help. They just wanted him to know that they wouldn't be back to the group, not together at least. And they weren't.

Maybe we're too frightened by other people's storms. Maybe we fear that if other people are embarrassingly honest about where or when they've cracked up and crashed, debris all over the sand and the rudder stuck way up in the trees, they might expect us to be equally honest. And our debris isn't for public show, thanks.

Or maybe we assume it's none of our business. And sometimes it isn't.

But sometimes it is. Sometimes it's the arms around us that can hold on when our own hands have slipped from the ropes and we're going down.

A Love with One Powerful Grip

There has been in my life a Love that will not let me go. By that I mean God, not Todd—though Todd, he's held on too. But what I really mean here is Jesus.

I once liked to think that I was part of the sophisticated, educated, spiritually upgraded class of people who are Unobjectionably Broad and Religiously Vague, who speak of Divine Force or Spirit, lest we offend.

But what I really am is a hillbilly East Tennessean from a pretty little mountain, a nearly pathologically shy soul who writes because much of my life I've been too timid to speak, and whose spirit, not through any of my own doing, has always and everywhere thirsted for God—which is different from saying I've always and everywhere lived like it. I lost the Tennessee twang after years of living in Boston, and the hillbilly core has been lightly veneered with some academic degrees. But the faith and the love that grew with me in the land of red clay and white lightning got its hold on me young. And it's never, *never* let me or mine go.

So when I say, in my best veneered words, that circumstances in my hurricane seasons took turns for the better, you can know that those turns had a center. A hub. A Love with a powerful grip. I could say Higher Power here, or Über-Spirit, or some Emersonian Over-Soul in the hopes that my books could sell in the funky, overstuffed bookstores where I love to drink tea and read—and so my friends in Boston and the Bay Area could just once buy a book I'd written and not have to hide it in brown paper. But Over-Soul is not what I mean.

Because in the end, I asked for a change. From myself, my husband, our marriage, our parenting, my work, his work, how it all fit together—and how it didn't.

If Jesus makes such a difference, I'd told him, *then let's see the change.*

And Todd has had cause to hurl down the same gauntlet to me.

Part of our healing came from making concrete changes: we relocated so we could refocus our professional callings, limit our professional hours, hold close our family, and make a fresh start.

In the end, I've had to change as much as my husband. For both of us, our own sins and the repentance and forgiveness that's followed have lasered away the grudge-scars from the past.

These days, one sometimes hears forecasters of doom who pronounce that career women threaten the fabric of family cohesion. And certainly, there's danger in any lives too busy for investing well in relationships. But in Todd's and my experience, the growth of our individual senses of professional calling, as well as our learning to affirm and support each other, strengthened our marriage and family. As it turns out, I had the inner fortitude of a garden slug: a mere salting of criticism and I was oozing my insides all over the floor. My growing in my sense of calling, my God-giftedness, helped me to also grow as a person—and as a wife and mother— and helped me to live up to, and perhaps one day out of, the lurking low self-esteem and insecurities capable of causing so much damage to myself and others.

I can tell you this: I have lived *change*—heard it and felt it and watched it and held it. And it was change asked for—okay, maybe demanded—and received from us both that took us to an entirely new place, a new depth of love between us. A more intentional way of managing the little frictions that come with families working and loving and living together. A closeness like never before.

My second husband, I call him, in his second marriage to his second wife— though we're all the same people. Only we're different. Far stronger, far wiser, far more supportive of each other's work, far more gentle, far slower to anger. We have a far more passionate, laughter-filled, sleep-deprived marriage than I could have ever dreamed of—or prayed for.

But then, I hadn't been the only one praying.

In the end, I learned a courage to call out the best in someone I loved, just as he did of me. I learned from a hard, gruesome look at myself that taught me of grace.

In the end, we dove for the mast and righted the boat.

In the end, there were harbors and nets.

In the end, there was a God who once held out a hand to assassins, prostitutes, battered victims, and thieves and said, *Today you're starting over. Come sit by me and eat.*

It was the same God I'd known for years, only now he was waiting with a seat saved at the table for me.

In the end—what can I say?—there was Jesus. Jesus through friends and unspoken prayers and fully undeserved mercy. And so in the end, there was a beginning.

Grace

"You know," I told my friend Ginger after the crises were over and the happy, heady, rebuilding years were well underway, "I've learned that I can be a real pig and a brute."

"Well," Ginger insisted, refusing to relinquish her role as her friend's staunch protector. "Well," she said, "it's just…"

"Grace." That was what popped out of my mouth.

But that sounded too simple. Both of us had, after all, graduate-level theological degrees. We've discussed dense, complex books—between chick flicks.

I tried again. "It's just… You'd think by now, I would've… I never knew before just how…" I looked at her helplessly, waiting for the decades of our friendship to fill in words I couldn't find—old friendships can do that.

She stopped walking. Nodded slowly. And hugged me.

Maybe one of us mouthed the word *grace*.

Maybe it didn't need saying out loud.

Mommy, Daddy, babies.

A Slowing-Down Season

When the Time Comes to Step Back Together

N ow before I say unkind things about Boston, let me first say that it's my all-time favorite American city. And if you've not visited it or been lucky enough to live there, you must at this moment raise your right hand and promise that you will not let another birthday go by before making plans to see Bean Town—with two mandatory pilgrimages: (1) the Freedom Trail and (2) ancient, irreplaceable Fenway Park and the Green Monster to see God's own team, the Sox, play.

That said, there's a dark side to dear Boston. I once read a study exploring which of the largest U.S. cities was the most fast-paced. Researchers took into account, as I recall, such hard data as the speed at which pedestrians walked and at which vehicles attempted to wend their way through traffic and how many nanoseconds could pass after a light turned green before the second driver in line made full use of a horn. The winner? Dear, quirky Boston, home of the bean and the cod—and the candle burned at both ends.

And not only does the city's pace of life exceed the sonic boom, but there's a peculiar pride that goes along with living like that: *My name's Ben and I'm a student at The Law School (the word "The" in Boston means Harvard) and The Graduate School (remember, it's always Harvard); here's my curriculum vitae if you'd like to peruse it, and, oh yes, I'm perfecting my French—on tape, you know—as I run every day…* And this was just introductions during coffee-doughnut hour at our church.

During the one unremarkable year I served as a Baptist chaplain at The University, I once sat through a United Ministry meeting in which someone mentioned that we all needed to be watchful of suicidal tendencies among our students—there'd just been a tragic case of a graduate student in the sciences. She added that, in fact, Harvard was not first in student suicides nationally but actually second to Rice University in Texas. And I tell you the truth, the initial reaction of the whole room was overachiever outrage. *What? Not first? What kind of shoddy research…?*

It's a sickness, I tell you. An infectious disease. And both my husband and I suffered from it severely. When our ludicrously talented friend Ray Hammond was admitted to a local hospital for exhaustion, Todd and I confessed to each other that we felt—after hearing that Ray was okay—spasms of time-efficiency envy, thinking, *I must not be getting nearly as much done as he is.*

More sane, self-disciplined people could have stayed in a place they loved, among people they loved, and dropped an anchor somewhere. We, on the other hand, needed help. By that I mean divine assistance and also a structural change, since God works through what's around us and what isn't: you don't set up cots for alcoholics in a tavern. A job offer for my husband was a chance to start over and rethink our lives, now that our lives included a child—and, who knew, maybe more children one day.

There was hope for calm, we thought, in a rural town outside of Charlotte, North Carolina, where I could buy alfalfa at the one-store crossroads. In Boston, we'd both taught college classes, both worked as ministers, both worked on graduate degrees, and started a family—our little boat was so heeled over we were taking on water, and fast. Alfalfa was looking very appealing.

It broke our hearts to leave New England, where we'd been a part of a scrappy urban church with a grand total of one parking place and even so, fewer and fewer empty pews. Our congregation had lived through the early years of one another's courtships and marriages, the births of the first children, the overflow for the first time in decades of the musty old nursery. Young and without extended family nearby, we'd been there for one another through the good, bad, and disastrous.

But God was pulling my little family in a different direction. Todd and I had faced some hard truths about ourselves, the structure of our relationship and the structure of our days, and we were committed not just to righting what had capsized but also to learning how to live far better, far more kindly and well together. We were committed to growing not just a good but a marvelous marriage. And we were finding that the healing and reworking we needed, unlike the grad school papers we'd both been known to churn out, couldn't be done in a weekend with late-night assistance from Domino's.

A Final Lap in the Fast Lane—for a While

As if Todd and I needed to prove to ourselves how far beyond manageable our lives had become, our last weekend in Boston—fewer than forty-eight hours before movers would show up at our house—we were expected in Litchfield, Connecticut, to co-officiate at the wedding of Kendall and Marianne, close friends and parishioners at our Cambridge church. Sensible people would have done the math on the rooms that were not packed and subtracted the number of hours left between Connecticut and the moving van and politely declined the invitation to the wedding. But we were not, nor are we now, very sensible people.

The bride had thoughtfully taken the time to arrange child care for our two-year-old daughter so that Todd and I could go over the joint homily together before changing from shorts into something more befitting the background of nuptial pageantry. I'm happy to report that the bride showed up for her part in the wedding. Her friend appointed to child care, however, did not—at least not at the agreed-upon time so we could serenely, meditatively prepare and change clothes. I was barefoot—which is not unusual for me except that I do typically wear shoes for weddings—and in khaki shorts and a Red Sox T-shirt in a losing season. (They were all losing seasons back then.)

I should add here a small detail. Marianne had grown up Catholic, and though she'd been an active member of our Protestant congregation in Cambridge, she cherished the upbringing that had first brought her to faith. To honor that, she understandably wished to hold the wedding in her hometown and in her home church and with her home priests. Along with—and here was the teensy-weensy catch—the husband and wife on staff at the church where she and Kendall had met.

"One of the priests," she mentioned offhandedly, "is not pleased with a woman's participation in the wedding ceremony." She smiled.

"Wait...um, wait." In any personality assessment, my score careens toward the end of the spectrum of People Pleaser and then hurls itself off the end of the chart. "So this guy doesn't want me to participate?"

Under the time crunch—avalanche really—of trying to sell a house, buy a house, pack a house, keep a toddler from unpacking a house, and buy a car, the homily was still in a state of disrepair. Here I was to co-officiate in a wedding—in a T-shirt and no shoes. We had no child care for our more-than-active toddler. And the clerical home team wasn't wild about the looks of me—on principle, that is, shoes or no shoes.

Todd and I had already begun to snap at each other over the homily, which was, no doubt, something profound and edifying on being patient and gentle with each other, loving as Christ loves...

When someone finally emerged to serve as sitter, we handed off our toddler-treasure and tore for the back of the sanctuary, where rumor had it there was a room that would do for changing. As we dove in, I noticed a small plaque over the door that read Reconciliation Room. Todd and I began shedding sweaty T-shirts and reaching for neckties and pantyhose, respectively, before we'd so much as swung the door all the way shut. I'd forgotten, I quickly realized, to bring a slip to go under the peach dress the bride had requested I wear rather than a clerical robe.

And so I burst from the room zipping the zipper that had snagged halfway up my back, toting my shoes in one hand, and tugging on the rayon skirt of the dress that clung to the hose in the absence of any slip.

An older woman stood waiting outside the door. She looked me up and down and audibly gasped, which I thought a bit odd.

"I am looking," she announced icily, "for the Reconciliation Room."

The zipper was still very much stuck, despite my best tugs, but I stopped just short of asking the woman to help. "Oh, well, you've found it. Right here."

I released the zipper tag long enough to point to the sign over the door.

"Is there," she asked, her eyes narrowing, "a *priest* in that room?"

She was looking down now at my legs, too much of which I realized were showing.

I tugged down the skirt.

"Oh," I laughed, suddenly realizing what she must have thought. "Oh, heavens no. No, goodness, there's nothing but a Baptist preacher in there."

Happy to have relieved the woman's suspicious mind, I yanked one last time on the zipper as I wheeled around and ran smack into Father O'Malley. Who scowled. At me. And my clingy peach skirt and my pantyhosed feet and my arm hooked over my shoulder and down my back, where the zipper still clung to its strip of wayward rayon. And his eyes met, I could see, those of the older woman, who looked very pale—whatever pale happens this side of a stroke. It occurred to me then that my assurance of the Baptist preacher with me in the Reconciliation Room might not have helped as much as I'd meant for it to.

"Hello," I said meekly to him, "um, Father." I began walking away, then turned, thinking I might explain—about the baby-sitter not showing up, about our changing at the last minute, about the rush with the homily...

About the crunch of our lives, the move and the stress and all the boxes not packed and...

About why there was a two-year-old girl in his church's foyer happily and loudly inquiring, "Are my mommy and daddy finished marrying yet?" About why I *still* wasn't wearing shoes.

About how *someone* in my marriage—maybe *everyone* in my marriage—had to slow down. And how this was the beginning of our trying to do that.

How did he think we were doing so far?

But there was no good place to go after the *um, Father.* So I saw him again only as the four of us stood at the front of the church: Father O'Malley and Father O'Toole, in black priestly raiment and clerical collars, and my husband, in a dark suit, and me, the dishwater blonde in peach rayon.

The ceremony began. At the back of the church, I could see the curls of our little goblin-fairy bounce by every so often. But I tried to focus.

From both priests, I heard searing words of grace and peace that I believed, too. And I listened to Todd, this man I'd not liked much about an hour ago as we argued, this man I'd vowed these very words to, this man I adored.

And with dignity and respect, the priests listened to Todd's words and then to mine.

And two people, who, if they're human, would feel many days very much like *two*, became *one*.

I remember few details from the wedding itself, except the gleaming faces of bride and groom. I remember all of us on the clerical Not-So-Dream Team hugging one another and Todd and I asking each other's forgiveness.

My favorite picture from that day shows Todd and me, our older daughter in our arms, with two kindly older men laughing beside us: our new-best-friend-Irish-Catholic-priest-coworker buddies. The picture sits on our sideboard, five relocations and five thousand cardboard boxes later. And sometimes as I pass by, I'm reminded of the Reconciliation Room—that was, in fact, what it proclaimed. Though I never explained about the baby-sitter. About my forgetting a slip. Or about how desperately we were needing a slowing-down season…

And I'm reminded of the uncomfortable circles of work and partnership God tosses us into so we can learn about grace. And respect. And the Spirit who shows up even when we're not entirely there ourselves.

And a God who guides us on how to let the sails luff just a little and cut down—whatever the cost—on a speed of life that's begun to threaten the health of our spirits, our insides, or who we are as a family.

A *Green Acres* Era

So our North Carolina microfarm, as our neighbor Dale called our sprawling 1.7 acres, was to be our solution.

We were a living rerun of the old sitcom *Green Acres,* only reversed, with my husband as the city dweller who never gets why the man unloading our garbage at the dump—no trash pickup service this far out in the country—wanted to trade howdies and chat. That would make me the wannabe farmer with the pitchfork and the silly grin.

The family plan was that Todd and I would each limit ourselves to one career. In his case, this meant college chaplaincy. In my case, this meant finishing a doctorate and publicizing a book. At the time, we had only one child. And only one dog and one cat. And later one retiring racehorse.

It seemed like a good plan.

It *was* a good plan.

It allowed us to work on our marriage and to come up from the depths of perpetual motion where we'd lived for so long.

A relocation or radical shift in jobs truly can help in starting over and redefining our days. But in our case, it soon became clear that two things we'd packed with us that we should've left back in New England were—the two of us.

We'd found the enemy, and it was staring at us from the other side of the bed. And also from the mirror over the sink.

Slowly, we began unlearning old habits of too-hasty words and hurt feelings that nobody had time to talk out. Slowly, we crafted new patterns that included good work and good play, time to sit in the gazebo and watch the horses graze and feel the southern sun and taste the sweet tea—and on a bad day with big winds, smell the turkey farms not far away.

It was a good time of learning and of focus. And essential to our approaching our next season with a little more wisdom than we'd had in the last.

A Slowing-Down Season for Strategizing

Get any random group of working-age parents together and bring up the subject of child care and work and just watch the anxiety level in the room swell like floodwaters. *Should I push for working only three days a week? Would our family budget survive? My husband despises his job and I adore mine, but he makes more money, so if anyone's going to cut back... My wife's job is the one with the best medical benefits, and given our kids' particular needs, we can't do without...*

Sandra Day O'Connor took a few years off from practicing law to stay home with young children, and it didn't collapse her career ladder. In fact, she's often trundled out as the poster mom for staying home with your kids. Good for her. Except...look into her life a little more deeply and the story is more multilayered than her baking cookies all day for each of those years.

She graduated from law school at Stanford and bore her first child three days after she passed the state bar exam. The woman has smarts *and* impeccable timing.

O'Connor opened her own law firm during that child's first year of life. At the birth of her second of three sons, she did leave the firm but became vice chairwoman of her county's Republican Party and president of the Junior League, her city's premier social-status group for women. She then ascended quickly in the ranks of state politics as she gave large parties and worked on Barry Goldwater's presidential bid.[1]

Now law school and political networking may not be a part of our years at home with our kids. But O'Connor's choices do pose an interesting question: perhaps a season at home can be part of strategic career plotting.

My since-early-childhood chum, Susan Bahner Lancaster, is the kind of literature professor the students carry out on their shoulders at the end of each class: a happily-ever-after kind of *Dead Poets Society.* She's worked full time and part time and is currently staying home with her youngest child. And while she misses teaching, it's clear she feels secure in what she's chosen for now. And I love hearing her dream about what might lie up ahead. The disabilities of her beloved brother Tabb, who died a few years ago, have spurred her serving on nonprofit boards serving the disabled. Perhaps, she muses sometimes, a career with a nonprofit…

> Staying home with a little one, or even bigger ones, is very like abandoning the rat race for the hamster wheel. When I relinquished a place in the work-with-a-pay-stub-force for work in the home, I found that life can quickly collapse into an endless round of laundry, diapers, sports practice, and cooking, and at the end of the day, it can collapse into simply collapsing. And yet, there are all of the payoffs a lifetime of smarmy TV has taught me to expect: sticky kisses and fierce hugs and the occasional jaw-dropping insight about life. Another upside is the chance, however infrequent, to contemplate the next career choice. Sure, staying home—knee-deep in board books and exponentially expanding numbers of Lego pieces—doesn't seem like a sabbatical from a career, but it is a sabbatical nonetheless. There are days enough to let an idea germinate and grow, days to think about what comes next in my life.… It is a rare opportunity I have—to be thoughtful about the next step, all the while being showered with art projects involving glitter and macaroni.

A season of time off or part time away from work outside the home can be invaluable—for *both* kids and career.

When a Parent Needs Picketing

For Andria Hall, former weekend anchor for CNN, the call to a new season of life came when family and career collided one day in her own home.

Raised by civil rights activists who infused in her both professional ambition and devotion to God, she attributes part of her career success and spiritual and emotional health to the community of faith and the role models around her: "My next-door neighbor was the first African American woman to run for president of the United States. It was nothing for my grandmother to say, 'Now you run this pie over to Ms. Chisholm...'"

And with Hall's father deeply involved in the civil rights movement of the 1960s, "Uncle Martin" was a regular guest in their home. "You know the pictures of Martin Luther King Jr.?" she asks, beaming. "And the March on Washington, and all the leaders are there on the steps of the Washington Monument beside him? My dad's there in that picture."

But in his calling to the civil rights movement, "my dad was rarely at home," she recalls. "So my sister and I decided one time to picket." Sticking poster board to big sticks, they welcomed him home from jail one day with signs that read:

Daddy stay home.
We need you here!
Fight for OUR rights.
    —Your daughters

She laughs. "And he did for a while. Children can be the ultimate reality check."

But the prayer and the smarts and the background and the hard work that got her in front of an international camera also meant she was constantly on the road in her own career, with three children at home: "I was commuting—four to five days in Atlanta, two to three days in New Jersey—trying to balance, trying to juggle."

Then one day when she'd been home for just a couple of days and was headed back to Atlanta for the week, she called in to her youngest son, who yelled, "Bye, Mommy," without so much as looking up from the television. Her daughter called down from upstairs, a distracted, "Oh...bye, Mom." And her middle son, Cameron, came crawling across the floor, grabbed hold of her coat and cried, "Mommy, don't go! *Mommy, don't go!*"

She shakes her head. "That was *my* picketing. That was the voice of my son crying out in the wilderness saying, *Mommy, what about me?*"

She resigned from CNN, began her own consulting firm, and continued her speaking and writing career on her own. A risk. But all more fitting for her season of life. A slowing down—for a season. A chance to redirect the ship.

Time for Compromise

In our case, the picketing came in the form of a little boy's tears.

All that marital goodwill in North Carolina produced another baby, a precious son, the ultrasound told us.

And all that time to focus on our work—each of us with one career, not several—had made us feel better prepared for whatever lay up ahead.

Only "up ahead" came flying at us fast.

Before I'd even delivered, our North Carolina microfarm was on the market, and we were buying six acres in China Spring, Texas. A university had come wooing my husband, and the job had seemed too right to turn down.

This was supposed to be part of the same plan we'd had when we moved to North Carolina and resolved to do what we both felt most called to do. Though, even squinting at it, it didn't look much like slowing down.

Together, Julia and I celebrated our graduations—kindergarten and a PhD, both of us ecstatic—with a party thrown by her godparents. But feeling out of place and far from home in Texas, I began letting pace replace focus. Just as soon as finished my dissertation, I was back to teaching and writing again. This time two jobs with two children. Our son, Justin, had just turned one.

Julia, social and precocious, had always loved outside child care, and we assumed all children raised by us would react the same way. But Justin, cuddly, sweet, and artistic, grouped all places in two categories—Home and Not Home—and all people into two categories—Mom and Not Mom. He was enrolled in the most state-of-the art child-care facility in our city—a working parent's dream, with a gorgeous, shaded playground and a stable, long-tenured, highly educated staff and a low teacher-child ratio and bright, clean, colorful rooms where happy children crafted Neuschwanstein Castles out of blocks. Julia, who had been there for pre-K, adored it.

But Justin wept.

Morning after morning.

I wept. In the observation room. On my way to teach. In the child-care facility director's office.

The director, a kind and intelligent woman, gently leaned across her desk to me. "You know, children pick up on our ambivalences. If Justin senses you don't feel entirely good about leaving him, he will conclude this must not be a good place to be."

Once again, it was the mother's fault. Of course. All of life that does not go as we hope is the mother's fault.

This was not what the kind and intelligent day-care director intended me to get from our talk; it was just what I heard.

"If, on the other hand," she suggested, "you leave him each day with confidence and enthusiasm, he will quickly understand that this is a good place to be."

"That makes sense," I said. Because it did.

Then I did the only mature, courageous adult thing to do: I turned tail and asked my husband to drop Justin off at the center.

Things improved, slightly, yet still the tears fell.

We sat down to discuss our choices—thankful that unlike so many families, we did indeed have some choices.

Justin needed more time at home. That was something we wanted to give him, and both of us wanted to spend more time with our children. Yet, in that way we can all embrace utterly contradictory goals and still imagine that we're rational human beings, neither of us particularly wanted to take time off from our work.

The bottom line, though, was that I *did* have the immense luxury of teaching only on Tuesdays and Thursdays; grading and preparation could be done from a home office. Because I was writing many hours a week, I'd not vied for a tenure-track position yet. The bad news was that I was being paid Victorian chimney-sweep wages. The good news was that it offered tremendous flexibility, both for writing and for time with my kids. And I had a husband who viewed the care and feeding of children equally as his delight and his dilemma, along with mine. Todd, though concerned about Justin, was a faithful, ferocious watchdog of my career and the number of hours I had to write and to teach.

We withdrew Justin from the center.

This was in no way related to how highly I viewed the director's advice or the lovely shaded playground. There was no doubt I was feeling Justin's desire to stay home, and Justin was feeling the conflict duking it out in me.

But unlike many of my friends and colleagues, I did have some choices about ways to keep working and still give Justin more of what he apparently craved—although it involved more late nights and excessive caffeine consumption on my part and more cooking and cleaning on the part of my husband.

We had learned during our days in Boston that sometimes the best remedy for a relationship that is less than healthy is simply more time. Time to address what is off-kilter. And time has to come from somewhere; it has to be withdrawn from someone's account. It's never lying around loose and ready for the taking.

Harsh but True Reality of the Adult World #452: sometimes two good goals are not achievable at the same time. Which means this may be a season for being creative or for compromising. Or for preparing for the next season. For making some tough choices.

So I began teaching less than I might have liked, but writing more, which I loved and could do from home. And Justin thrived.

For many of us, to call these career and parenting questions complex is like calling Kilimanjaro a rise in the road. What works for one family simply can't for another. For one family, a slowing-down season can be used for reestablishing focus: *What was it we were both passionate about in these professions in the first place?* Or making a change: *Is there something else I ought to be preparing to do?* Or strengthening family bonds: *I have all evening to hear about what you're thinking, and I can't wait.*

But slowing down doesn't have to mean completely dry-docking your professional life.

Even as the debate over whether a woman can take time from her career for family without committing professional suicide has reached a fever pitch, Meredith Vieira provided an intriguing example. Having quit a very prestigious, very enviable, and very grueling position with *60 Minutes* fifteen years ago in order to spend more time with her husband and three children, she was offered a new stint with NBC's *Today* show. With, reports suggest, a salary of ten million dollars.[2] She seems to have come back rather well.

My favorite used-book store in Texas was owned by a woman who'd wanted a business she could run with her four children roaming the aisles. And she ran it so well that her husband, an attorney who wanted more time with his kids, quit his job and joined her.

And in a small town near me live a husband and wife who'd dreamed of spending more time with their kids and living on a charming main street above the shop they own and run—which they made a reality, and now produce some of the finest chocolate in the Southeast.

For all of us, the arrival of children means shifted priorities and time commitments—and interests and passions in areas we never thought twice about just a few years ago. And sometimes that leads us to a season of sea-change adventures.

Launching New Journeys

For us, that adventure was an adoption. By the time my husband and I reached serious thoughts on adopting a child, we'd prayed long and hard over what a third child might do to our careers and to the two older children. I'd already decided that teaching could go for a while if it had to, just as long as I could write some healthy portion of every day.

And then, after we had filed small rain forests worth of paperwork, we found ourselves discussing another thousand-mile move. Granted, the move looked appealing on many levels, but the timing was nuts. Was nuts *again*, I should say, since clearly this was a pattern for us.

In fact, we were standing in the Dallas/Fort Worth Airport on our way to visit the potential new city of residence when the adoption agency called Todd's cell to say we should be ready to leave for China two days after Thanksgiving. When a girlfriend called my cell moments later, I begged her, "So, please, until I get back from this trip, please, whatever you do, just *don't* look at your calendar and tell me how long that is away."

"But it's just a week and a half from today!"

Like me, my friends don't always listen too well.

"I need," I explained, "to live in delusion for a few days. Until we know if this job thing will work out and whether the moving van will be pulling up to our house the same day we fly back from the other side of the planet. Okay?"

We knew we were flying to Asia to embrace a little girl who'd been in an orphanage since the age of two weeks. We suspected it was time for another slowing-down season.

But in our typically chaotic way of preparing to slow down, we ran crazed. In the midst of packing to visit China and move outside Texas—equally foreign by Lone Star standards—we attempted to sell a house and buy a house and prepare the older kids for the move and the new baby sister.

What we didn't foresee, among so many things, was falling in love with our new daughter's country of birth. The deep river gorges and finger-shaped mountains, Tang-dynasty poetry and red pagodas and imperial palaces, carved jade, and embroidered silk… We were enthralled.

And maybe, having never been adoptive parents before, we didn't foresee exactly how it would feel to meet our new daughter, our Jasmine. Crazy in love with a gorgeous bundle of creature. Nutty, irrational, here-have-a-kidney-oh-and-both-of-my-lungs kind of love. After too many weeks between her picture and her touch, she could rest in our arms.

We nine families whose daughters came from the same orphanage sat silently, our babies bundled in our arms, as our bus wound through town to the spot where each of our daughters had been found the previous winter, some wrapped in a blanket or a piece of carpet, some with a bottle and bit of formula tucked inside, two in the open-air market, one outside a school, one outside the police station. It was a bus ride to make you reorder your life minute by minute.

Over the growl of the bus, we spoke of what had brought us all here, what had already slowed down or sped up or given way to make room for this moment: our shifting work schedules, our older children, the backyard swimming pool one family decided not to build so they could use the savings for the adoption. We had each entered a restructuring season.

Back in the States, our two older children met for the first time the baby sister they already loved. That very first night, just a few days before Christmas, the three children played peekaboo into the wee morning hours, and Jasmine, the formerly quiet and fearful child, laughed until she shook.

Sometimes, it seems, a slowing-down season can make way for the arrival of joy.

Time Out of Joint

Three weeks later we celebrated the birth of our Christ and Jasmine's first birthday—events forever linked in my mind, one made possible by the other.

And within that same three weeks, we had moved.

We'd begun a still-different season as a family of five in a new land. Time was out of joint. And we were glad.

We certainly didn't foresee the intensive care unit we'd be running soon after the move. Having left in early January for Tennessee, where we'd not yet found a house, we proceeded to stash two adults, three children, and more four-legged creatures than Todd ever thought he'd tolerate in his lifetime in a two-bedroom apartment that quickly shrank to about twenty-two square feet. Various members of the family—all but baby Jasmine, our immunological rock—then proceeded to contract mono and parvo and strep throat and vesicular stomatitis, usually limited to cattle, horses, and swine but in this case including my family. We saw every medical specialist we could find but a large-animal vet, and clearly, we should have started with the vet.

We became our own containment area.

The kids missed a total of five weeks of school. It seemed like fifteen.

I valiantly attempted to homeschool them in the midst of their illnesses. But it turns out that homeschooling for me looks like packing the kids in the van to Barnes & Noble, where I buy everyone hot chocolates in the café and we all sit and read. Left to my version of homeschooling, no child in my family would be able to count.

But this slowing-down season, enforced by disease and bad winter weather and a tiny apartment, was a strangely wonderful bonding experience. Not the hacking coughs or the scary 105-degree fevers or the interminable waits for Vanderbilt doctors to see if we'd somehow contracted our own new form of swine flu, but the day after day of being together. Above all, there was Jasmine; her addition to our family was pure delight.

And the timing was right, at least for a season, for a less-harried rhythm to our days. Todd and I could focus more—on better parenting for both of us, on more writing than teaching for me, and on a new role in a good place for Todd.

We watched as the older kids' physical, emotional, and spiritual health improved daily. The behavioral issues we'd battled in Texas—never dire but often distressing—smoothed out, some disappearing entirely.

Stricken, I called several states away to a friend who is doggedly loyal to me *and* familiar with my many faults.

"I have terrible news," I announced.

She gasped into the phone. "Are the kids all ri—?"

"Fine. Never better. That's just it," I wailed into the line. "It's as if," I lowered my voice to a whisper, "there's some kind of relationship between time spent disciplining our children and their behavior!"

For everything there is a season, including a season for slowing down. For growing more intentional in our *becoming*—as parents, as professionals, as people of faith. For focusing not just on our individual callings but also on our journey together.

Jasmine prompted that shift, that new rhythm of life. Jasmine—along with medical desperation—brought us that wisdom along with the precious gift of herself.

By now, the hideously swollen glands and lips have shrunk, the numb appendages are revitalizing, and the oozing sores have scabbed over. We're trimming the sails and gaining speed again, but we're conscious of remembering, *honoring*, what we've learned during these seasons of babies and moves and newness and sickness and health and change.

We're welcoming visitors to our home again now, so come see us.

We'll keep the light—and the fumigator—on for you.

Taking Turns at the Tiller

Relocating for Your Spouse's Work—and It Hurts

Perhaps you've picked up on a subtle theme of Todd's and my three-career marriage: relocation. One of the heartbreaks of my adult life, in fact, has been the many relocations we've made, the grief of driving away with a full car and a full heart and nothing certain but trust in the God of a murky tomorrow. And even that trust falters at certain turns, the sorrow so sharp it flails the breath from you.

Several years ago, I found myself in a small group of couples in which we were asked to describe ourselves in botanical terms. I was sitting cross-legged on the floor and thinking of having my roots recently yanked from where they'd become entwined with friends and extended family. I chose as my image a small potted tree from Home Depot that had been transplanted three too many times, whose roots had nowhere to reach but concrete and plastic, and whose spindly trunk blows over in a strong wind.

I know too well what it's like to be in the throes of buying a house and selling a house and examining schools and wincing from the thousand shards of answers that never quite piece together into the sweet, affordable, abundant square-footage bungalow with the short walk to the park and the easy commute and the vast, mountain-view acreage and the Starbucks on the corner.

Yet one of the greatest treasures of my adult life has been the new friendships that have sprouted in alien soil and continue to flourish long distance. Oceans and mountains and many time zones between us, and still the e-mails and phone calls find their way back and forth, asking, "How's your heart? How's the kids' new school working out? Are you finding God somewhere in this next stage of your work? Is it still snowing there? How is your *heart*?"

This isn't the first era of couples leaving family and friends and the familiar to start a new life in a strange land—clearly, the covered-wagon crowd knew the risks of relocation. But ours is an era of pioneering the three-career kinds of moving-or-not decisions. Does the family's location always follow the person who currently makes more money? Or does the hard-to-place profession take precedence in job searches? If one person's work can be practiced almost anywhere, does he or she get as much say in where the family goes? When do the demands of aging parents insist that two professional people limit the scope of their potential moves to a certain region?

In this sense, you and I and our colleagues and friends are sailing uncharted seas—Columbus with better medical benefits.

Spilled-Open Lives

In the midst of working on this chapter, I sent a brief e-mail to a select group of these friends who'd moved in recent years either for their spouses' callings or their own.

"Tell me about the process," I asked them. "How do you and your spouse make relocation decisions? Can you tell me what's been good, bad, wrenching, rewarding, horrific?"

Maybe it was the lateness of the hour, catching too many of them in that children-tucked-in space of quiet when they could uncover memories or unwrap their thoughts about a new and not-easy season. But by the next morning, my inbox was overflowing with spilled-open lives. I began reading the messages one by one, just before taking my kids to school, and could hardly find my way above the wash of "Well, Since You Asked" to find my keys to the car.

Some of the more analytical types spoke with less emotion, a "just the facts, ma'am" approach to moves. These were the mathematical minds and computer-software consultants and finance professors. I value these friends because they're so refreshingly unlike me.

Sally, a mother of three and a physician, professor, and research director with an MD and PhD, was one of these. She and her husband, Joel, a religion professor, had recently moved to Texas for Joel's work. Sally had been unflappable about the decision: ready to stay, ready to move. She'd found a job in Texas that was a fine fit for her gifts and calling, caring for the medical needs of low-income families. When she e-mailed recently, it was to report in her usual unshakeable pleasantness that they were staying put for the time being: "We both now have what we believe are irreplaceable jobs here, but if we were to move, I suspect it would be for Joel to have a tenure-track position, and we'd only go somewhere that had a program for me." Easy, matter-of-fact, faithful as always.

But then there were the e-mails full of pain, mostly from the artists and actors and writers and ministers and humanities professors—the kind of people, like me, whose Rich Interior Lives drive everyone nuts, including themselves.

When Thanne, a speech pathologist, and I met, we bonded over both being in trailing-spouse shock, her having just left Seattle and my having just left New England and North Carolina in too-quick succession. Thanne's e-mail sat at the top of my inbox, letting me know that she and her husband, Steve, were on the cusp of a move again. Their oldest daughter would be a high-school senior the following year, and they'd just finished weeks of prayer and negotiations over a job offer for Steve in the Northwest, no less than a continent away. They'd been searching for possibilities to let the oldest daughter finish her final year and debating how a move might affect the youngest daughter and… As a couple and as a family, they'd come to the same place: Steve would take the job. And they'd walk with their children through whatever that meant for the family.

"But our feelings," Thanne said, "haven't yet caught up with our Yes."

Another response rolled in from Kelly Shushok, who is the minister of small groups at her church and a mother of three. In her work, she sometimes speaks to groups of young adults who, in fits of romance and piety, have been known to hold hands and say to her, "We just know that if we just pray hard enough, eventually

God will give us both the peace that passes all understanding and that's how we'll know it's the right decision."

But Kelly insists:

> I want to be the one who gives a countertestimonial…that every time we've ever moved (five times in ten years), I believe it's been the right decision. It has *not*, however, been accompanied with either peace or understanding by at least one of us. So trust is *huge*, and you have to admit when you're the one who is really unsure, and you have to go with the one who is pretty sure.… Ultimately, it really is who you are and not where you are…but who you are *together* trumps the whole deal.… It has really helped us that we *both* have chapters in our marriage we can point to and say, "Oh yeah, he/she sacrificed for me that time."

Her point is a crucial one—though we may not always want to hear it. Perhaps in the long run, "All will be well, and all will be well, and all manner of thing will be well," as the fourteenth-century mystic Julian of Norwich proclaimed. But getting to that "will" in Julian's words just might turn out to be the length of Interstate 10 and as full of potholes.

And in the short run, the gut-honest truth of the matter looks more like this: in certain seasons, after a decision to relocate is made *together,* one spouse or the other might simply have to go along for the ride, bouncing over the wake, and offer support and find what job he or she can whenever it arises, and might have to be mangy-dog *miserable* for a while. I don't know any nicer way to say it.

That's not to say God can't work through any situation. In the end, God might give the sacrificial, trailing spouse the job of his or her dreams or the longed-for time with children. It's not to say that goodness might not grow even in the land of self-denial, way west of Eden. But it's selling reality short to pretend that in the short run it will all turn out just peachy, with fulfillment and good salaries and killer job titles and sufficient vacation and access to extended family, plus amiable climate, good architecture, and abundant ethnic restaurants. For two people who both want to pursue a purposeful calling, at least one of which requires some relocation, and both want to prioritize the well-being of their children, such decisions simply *will* be complex, sometimes even painful. But in the long run, our families can learn and grow and find richness together, even in the land of cardboard moving boxes.

Happily Ever After...Except

Lots of us out there pay a heavy price for supporting our spouses in following their calling. We assure them we really do want them to go back to school even though there are three little mouths to feed. We pull a teenager out of her student council presidency to be the "new girl" in a strange land. We explain to our own colleagues that, no, we don't want to leave this job we love, but our spouse has been asked to...

Carole Pomilio, a speech pathologist from New Jersey and mother of three, knows a thing or two about a spouse's career shift. She reflected:

> My then-boyfriend had a career in the family business and was pretty successful.... Very soon after getting married, he decided he wanted to further his newfound career [as a painter] and needed to go to graduate school. So we decided together the best place to go is back to the college I graduated from. We were both young, in love, and incredibly naive. So there goes the moneymaking family business right down the tubes. And I have ever since been subjected to a life in the world of arts.... As crazy as that seems, I love my husband and want him to be happy.

Just tonight, I found my husband cleaning the kitchen as he laughed with a friend on the phone: Carole's husband, Mark. Mark just landed a terrific new job in Phoenix. And Carole's research credentials are such that she can be assured of getting a job, and a good one. Their two sons are fine with the move; their daughter, in high school, is understandably...not. Very much *not*.

"If you remember to pray for us...," Carole said.

Their feelings, I thought, remembering Thanne and remembering how I'd so often felt, *haven't yet caught up with their Yes.*

For Bruce Kuhn, a former Broadway actor, finding a soul mate came with major career *and* location ramifications. After years of confirmed bachelorhood, he'd found the woman of his dreams.

Happily ever after.

Except.

Bruce's work consisted of performing all over the United States. His clientele was based there. His connections.

Hetty lived in the Netherlands, a bicycle ride from the ocean where she rode to paint every day. Her clientele was based there. Her vision.

And they both wanted children.

Bruce recalls:

My artistic ambitions were the whole center of my universe. Then, by the grace of God, I met this *incredible* woman. I came to the point of saying, "I will purposely put you in front of myself," and she did the same.... She honors and respects my work enough to put her work on the line, and she's as committed to her artistic life as I am. I thought, *Wow, this could work.*

So at midlife, Bruce, who spoke not one word of Dutch or any other European language, hauled his worldly possessions a world away and replanted himself.

"Her clientele was more stationary than mine," he explains. "I lived in the Upper West Side of New York in a five-room apartment with four other guys." He chuckles. "She had this cottage on a dyke on an island in the North Sea in the south of Holland—*gee, where should we live?*" He shrugs, to say that decision of where to live was no contest. "But I don't think I understood how radically this would affect my artistic life."

Bruce rocks back in his seat at the memory of the culture shock of the first year of his marriage. He is both upbeat and brutally honest about their process. If the one decision of *where* to live was easy, he doesn't downplay the ongoing battle of the *how*—learning a new language and adjusting to a new culture at midlife or raising two children while one parent transatlantic commutes. In the same sentence, accompanied by the larger-than-life gestures and facial expressions that make him so good on stage, Bruce will tell you just how good—and how hard—those early years were.

And the truth is, *any* relocation is difficult, even when both spouses are in complete agreement about the decision, because moving your family means moving your soul, and replanting a soul—even in the richest of soil—takes time.

Deciding Whose Turn It Is Now

With new seasons come new opportunities to decide which career or family decision to put first—though it's not always easy.

When I first met Linnea and Joe Kickasola, they had just moved to Texas and were having dinner with a group of new faculty out near where I lived in China Spring. It was an outdoor dinner, with lovely white linen tablecloths and a gracious home and garden—and a temperature above one hundred degrees even after the sun had set. We were pigs on a spit in semiformal attire.

Joe had just been hired as a professor of communications at the university, my husband whispered to me as we crossed the lawn to greet them. Linnea was an opera singer who'd just spent the summer in Europe, where she'd had some encouraging breakthroughs. Her career was well on its way.

Though my mother tried to instill an appreciation of the art in me by playing *Carmen* in an endless loop on days when I'd be home sick from school, I know nothing about opera. Except maybe this: that it seems to happen in large urban centers in grand halls peopled by a class of people who own mink. Which would seem to make small-city, central Texas an unlikely place to launch a career.

"*Opera?*" I whispered back as we approached them. *"Does she understand where she's—"* And then it was time to shake hands and smile. She appeared sane enough. And determined.

But apparently it was indeed hard for Linnea to make progress in her profession in Texas. So Joe worked out a deal with the university to establish a program in New York for students of theater and film. Linnea and Joe moved to the Big Apple, where they're crafting a life with two place-specific professions and now also a toddler. I say bravo for them and their creative approach—bravo and roses tossed up on the stage.

African Methodist Episcopal Bishop Vashti Murphy McKenzie and her husband made a similarly bold move when their family structure changed. Early in their marriage, Vashti had shifted her career focus from journalist to fashion model to better accommodate her husband's life as an NBA basketball player. But when they began to talk about starting a family, she made it clear: "I'm not having a baby away from my mother."

She laughs now, "We didn't even pray about it. We just moved back to Baltimore. And my ministerial life has been so greatly enhanced by the presence of my parents—it's made all the difference."

When No One Knows Who You Are

In many relocations, the spouse without the exciting new job that precipitated the move has the more difficult adjustment, no matter how willingly he or she supports the other's career.

When my sister-in-law Beth, who loves big cities and all that they offer, left her job as a chaplain in DC, she followed my brother David to his new job as a pastor in a small southern town. For a few years, while the children were young, she worked only part time. Then, just as the youngest was headed to school, she was suddenly pursued by the job of her dreams two hours away. So David left a job he loved to scramble to find one in a city where he had few connections, where there were no guarantees.

So commitment to a three-career marriage does involve risk. And a great deal of mutual trust.

Part of the challenge of relocation, especially for the trailing spouse, can be the loss—or at least the severe disruption—of one's identity. My son has become fast friends with another six-year-old boy who recently moved here from Chicago. Billy's mother is kind and highly capable. But trotting each other's children back and forth between sleepovers, we'd appeared to each other primarily in sweats and T-shirts. As we sat together not long ago at a basketball game, she confessed the adjustment had been a surprisingly difficult one for her. The kids were doing beautifully. Her husband had some great opportunities.

But.

But she'd been the senior human resources officer in her corporation and had been responsible for an employee pool of more than thirty thousand. She missed her work.

"And it's just so odd," she confessed, "when no one knows who you are."

She added that she knew she was buying into our culture's idea that we *are* what we *do*—and that has nothing to do with God's vision for us. And yet...

And yet, she's right. It can be *hard.* Stripped of our power suits and flocks of employees, we're down to just being ourselves. Which sounds like a good spiritual discipline, and is—but that doesn't mean it feels just fine at the time.

Strangers in a Strange Land

It has always comforted me that at least one of the biblical psalmists also pined for a different place:

> By the rivers of [the Brazos] we sat and wept....
> There on the [mesquite]
>   we hung our harps....
>
> How can we sing the songs of the LORD
>   while in a foreign land?[1]

With only two little changes, we'd keened the same song, the psalmist and I.

For me, the toughest point in supporting my husband's professional calling came when we were living in North Carolina. I was pregnant with Justin. For the first time in our adult lives, we were within easy driving distance of extended family. It was our slowing-down season.

And that's when the large private university in Texas came hunting my husband.

"Texas?" I asked.

And while I couldn't argue with the university's excellent taste, and while the job description they faxed to us seemed written precisely for Todd, I was halfway through a pregnancy and my nest-building instincts were in full whirl. We'd just built and primed and painted a beautiful gazebo and a four-board wood fence around our home and landscaped ourselves into chronic back pain. Oh, and adopted that retired racehorse just off the track. (I do these things when I'm expecting, both biological pregnancies and adoptions, which is why three kids are probably enough.)

We could have said no to the move. Todd offered repeatedly to pull out of the process. But with the no-fly-zone approaching in my pregnancy's third trimester, I flew out to the heart of Texas to see if I liked it.

Now, Bostonians can be blue-blooded snobs, and I was part Bostonian— though admittedly light on the blue blood. Southerners, too, can be awfully provincial. What's the purpose of existence if you can't grow azaleas and get good sweet tea when you're out? I understand this. I'm part southerner, too.

But *Texas*?

This part of Texas was down I-35 from Fort Worth where, as Will Rogers said, the West begins and the East peters out. I could feel myself petering out there among the Honey-Who-Shrunk-the-Trees. In the middle of a drought unusual even for central Texas, it had not rained for months, and temperatures had scorched in the three-digit range for weeks.

I did not like the cactus-land. I did not like it, Sam-I-Am. I did not like the hot, dry west. I hoped to not with Texas mess.

But I refused to let my husband take his name off the list. And I watched, with not one blink of surprise, as his name stayed there as they whittled their list down from more than a hundred to a dozen and then four. It was too perfect for him, as if everything he'd done in his life from migrant farm-worker legislation to building latrines in South America and a Harvard degree suddenly all came into play. There was no question in my mind whether my husband would move for my sake if I'd been the one pursued for this job. A shame—if I thought even *maybe* he'd have held out on me, I could have chained myself to the magnolia I'd planted in our North Carolina front yard.

Instead, we listed a long line of items that would have to be true for us to know this was a go. They ranged from the crucial—the little university town *had* to have a National Public Radio station—to the completely goofy. But when the goofiest of the goofy checked out, one by one, I could read the handwriting on my fresh, white, four-board fencing: I'd been weighed in the balance and found wanted in Texas.

Or at least my husband had, and we planned to continue cohabitating.

The big, bad university asked my husband to come. Of course. With my full support, laced in grief, we said yes and prepared to pack a newborn, a preschooler, an eighty-pound golden retriever, a very mean cat, a retired racehorse, a postpartum pack of hormones, and two bone-weary adults into two sedans and drive west.

Now, choosing to move for the sake of your spouse's professional calling is implied but not exactly fleshed out in those outrageous marriage vows we utter.

There's nothing in the vows, I've since noticed, about cheerfully signing on for black widow spiders in your kids' sandbox or for rattlesnakes who think the warm, welcoming *Mi Casa Es Su Casa* sign hanging in your hall means *them*. There'd been nothing in the vows about fire ants in your newborn's wet diaper or cracks in the soil so wide your toddler's foot slips in and twists. Had someone mentioned in our wedding vows anything about the scorpion I'd find poised like a little brown lobster, tail set for a sting, on the hand holding my nursing baby's head, or tangled in my preschooler's hair, or skulking across the kitchen tile as my children ran bare-foot, it might have given me pause before I'd repeated the vows, there in the dog-wood-snow of a Tennessee spring.

For better, for worse.

"Um," I might have asked at the time. "Could you define that word *worse—* with concrete examples?"

"Scorpions," someone might have warned me. "The only creatures who walked away unscathed from the Nevada nuclear test sites. All through your house, all over your yard. And your neighbors will think this is *normal*."

But I didn't think to ask at the time.

One day when the largest of the creepy crawlies, sun spiders the size of a Texan's belt buckle, were playing Dance Dance Revolution on the front of my barn, I couldn't stop myself. I knew they weren't lethal and that they helped catch mosquitoes. I meant to smash only one with my broom—as an example to the rest. But the 111-degree day and the brown, crunchy lawn, and the clouds of locusts, and the howling of my very hot children, and my own sense of loss and isolation and regret welled up into my broom arm. Each spider splayed yellow blood in a nearly foot-wide circle.

I could not stop swatting.

My husband found me shell-shocked, mute, my wooden-handled weapon still clutched in my hand as I stared at where the massacre had washed yellow the wall of our barn.

"I think Mommy sort of lost it," my older child whispered to her father.

I did not like it in the sun. I did not like the scorpions. I did not like the Lone Star State. Not in a crate. Not with a mate.

But I knew, I *knew*—right through the spider blood on my barn—that we'd done the right thing to move. My husband loved his job, which was growing daily as he added new components. And, lonely as it was, I was finding the time to finish my dissertation. And on a few midnights when the baby was up and I couldn't bear the sight of another footnote just then, I even worked on a novel.

I missed my friends in New England and North Carolina and my extended family and my old job so much that it physically hurt. But I knew we were in the right place, at least for the moment. And I knew that, compared with women in most of the world, I—with healthy children and a husband who often *voluntarily* listened to feelings, a brave soldier of an air conditioner, and enough food for all the mouths milling around me—was unbelievably privileged.

As I slogged through my dissertation, made a few friends, learned to slide on my cowboy boots in one fluid motion, learned the names of the world champion rodeo bull riders, and admired the big sky sunsets that flamed over the live oaks and bluebonnets, I began to have spasms of This Ain't So Bad. And the native Texans were marvelous. Funny, down to earth, genuine, tough—expressing themselves in ways a writer would kill for: "He looked like ninety miles of bad road" and "She got herself another one of them Blue State dogs" (referring to the presumably liberal Yankees like me who owned a golden retriever).

Neighborhood gatherings featured mesquite-roasted barbecue venison and beef and great western music and storytelling, the men competing for who had the best recent rattlesnake confrontation: "They have a collective memory, you know them snakes do. So I couldn't kill that six-footer in my garage without giving him a decent burial. No sir. He's somebody's Uncle Alfonze, and they'll be coming to get me if..."

Two neighbors once lapsed into battle at one of these gatherings over the definition of a rattlesnake killing.

"I'm tellin' you, Tommy, I don't care how big it was, you can't count it as yours if you just ran over it in your truck."

"But I was the one who killed it. It was me."

"But you gotta shoot it or lasso it or hack it to death for it to count. Not run over it in a pickup the size of a house. I'm tellin' you, you can't keep this one as a trophy."

After these barbecues, or a particularly stunning sunset, I'd be carried away for a time on a wave of Maybe We Could Live Here Forever. Inevitably, though, one of those rattlesnake kills would take place a little too close to where our children played, or the fire ants would ambush me in bed over a crumb of brownie.

So some nights Todd and I sat up in bed—*not* eating brownies, as we'd learned the hard way—and dreamed of somewhere greener, but not warmer, somewhere that would offer me the job of my dreams and maybe a few gun-control laws.

In the meantime, I had to admit: the bluebonnets and Indian paintbrush under the live oaks and big sky in spring go on forever. And just as August in Texas was not exactly my favorite—when the sun seared my already withering garden—neither was April in Boston, when there had been snow still on our lawn. Besides, the National Cutting Horse finals at the Heart O' Texas Coliseum was my kind of evening out on the town.

And you can't live a day without knowing that life is a gift, every moment. A family together with each member liking one another—most of the time—is more precious than all the ideal locations, all the money, and all the nameplates on just the right office doors in all the world. Contentment and hard-won wisdom, I was learning, sometimes come along a journey you never wanted to make.

I'd moved away from my work, from our circle of extended family and friends, from the mountains and beaches I loved, all for my husband's job only because I was trying to listen to God and to love, honor, and cherish. I won't pretend I handled it with cheerfulness, good humor, or grace every day, because I didn't. And there were witnesses, and sun-spider blood on a barn to prove it.

In the short-run, there was no payoff for being the trailing spouse except a sensitive, understanding husband and the sense we both had of being where we needed to be for the time. Which didn't keep me from muttering, *How long, O Lord?* as I crushed another scorpion under my boot. Or from selling our home in the country to buy one in town, where lethal arachnids and things of a slithering nature were in shorter supply.

In the end, though, it is true what my friend Kelly said a couple of years after she left a job she adored in Maryland to relocate for her husband's job to a town she initially loathed. "No matter how full your moving truck is, God will find a way to squeeze in between your Christmas dishes and that plastic swimming pool you purchased three states ago. For this reason alone, you will be okay. Peace and understanding have always found their way back to us."

For us, too, peace and understanding did indeed find their way back. Though some days before that I was just sure I'd collapse by the side of the road waiting for peace and have scorpions build a nest in my bones.

And then, suddenly, we were preparing to move again, this time to a place that, for the first time, would feel like home to *both* of us from the start.

Yet, despite a long, hot season of my own discontent, a kind of spiritual desert, much of my own making, I'd come away wiser. And richer. As we set up camp with our new baby and two older kids in a temporary apartment in Tennessee, friends from back in Texas began sending baby gifts, e-mailing and calling with good wishes, and I was carried into the new place on a swell of gratitude for the past. Though I'd somehow never found my place in Texas, professionally or personally, I came away with a real affection for bluebonnets and big skies and for all those baby gift-givers, and for that dear Lone Star flag that even now—who would have guessed it?—flies in small scale in our Tennessee kitchen. And I'd come away grateful for life lessons learned, if even the hard way.

Where Help Comes From

Soon after our newly enlarged family of five—three of us just in from Hunan Province, China—arrived in middle Tennessee to house hunt, I sat in the passenger seat of our real estate agent's SUV on my way to tramp through yet another "Bright! Open! Airy!" floor plan.

It was the day before Christmas as the SUV climbed twisting two-lane roads tunneled over in silver limbs. Laura, our real estate agent, glanced over to the passenger seat, the ream of printouts of houses for sale untouched in my lap, my eyes on the woods and brimming.

"You okay?" she wanted to know.

I tried describing what I was feeling to her: "*Oh!*" I said, articulate as ever.

" 'Oh,' what? You sure you're okay?"

"It's just…these mountains…the snow…"

She shot me a look that told me these were not mountains, just nice rolling hills.

But, I wanted to say, if you'd been *raised* in the mountains and woods, had them infused into your soul, had them become part of how you saw God, and then been transplanted for years…

If you'd suddenly been given the chance to move closer to extended family just as your parents were facing health problems and needed your help and just as you'd adopted a child who needed to know more of family… If you'd seen the God of the orphans and aging up close just lately…

If you'd been given the incomparable gift of three incredible kids and of a husband whose gifts you admired so much you'd move to the ends of the earth for his sake, a husband who championed your work even when you'd lost all faith in yourself…

If you'd been learning these past few years so much more of a God who is momentously faithful, the one who stands firm, the one we run to and climb to and cling to…like the mountains I'd loved.

"It's just…," I said, my voice snagging on itself, "so…*beautiful.*"

I lift up my eyes to the hills, I was thinking, along with the psalmist. *Where does my help come from?*[2]

Here it was Christmas Eve, and I groped for something more holy, more theologically deep than my getting choked up about a big rise in the road.

"And I'm just so…" The top printout was smearing now, which must have meant I was crying. "So *grateful.* You know?"

She cut her eyes over at me one more time, shook her head, and shifted into first gear to crawl up the mountain—the *hill,* which was covered in hemlocks, their long graceful branches sequined in ice.

"Where does my help come from?" I wanted to say.

From the Lord God. Who walks with us through the desert. Who leads us by the still waters. Who restores our souls, even when there seems nothing left to restore.

From the Lord God. Maker of New Jersey and New England. Of Maryland and Manhattan. Of Holland and Hunan.

From the Lord God. Maker of heaven and earth. And, okay, maybe even of Texas.

When Work Is Away from Home Port

The Four Universal Laws of the Traveling Spouse

I took one physics class in college, which I think perhaps doesn't qualify me as an expert on thermodynamics. But there is some kind of relation, I'm sure, between the laws of thermodynamics and parenting. Now it goes against my nature to pronounce laws that apply to other people's lives, but here are four in the field of Traveling-Spouse Theory that I've crashed into along my own journey. I share them with you in the interest of fair warning.

Law of the Traveling Spouse #1

In families involving two professional parents, both parents holding jobs that require a good deal of traveling will be, at best, challenging if not impossible. It's a word I dislike—impossible—but there it is. Nannies and live-in grandparents might ease this situation, but for most of us, we need to approach our careers with the understanding that two professional parents can travel on business a little or one parent a little more, but the closer you come to a whole lot is pressing your luck, unless one of you chooses to stay home from work or bump down the hours for a time.

And this is partly because of…

Law of the Traveling Spouse #2

One of the laws of thermodynamics assures us that all matter is careening at all times toward chaos. (Am I remembering this right from college, or is this just my own household organization?) Similarly, it is a proven fact that when one spouse is traveling for work, the other currently-not-traveling-but-still-working spouse will more often than not experience at least one of the following: a mechanical malfunction in the central heat and air, minivan, refrigerator, or other essential device; a sick child or pet, usually with excessive vomiting involved; or a natural disaster. If the Traveling Spouse is in a particularly exotic location, the Guarding the Home Front Spouse may experience all of the above. At least one or all of the children may also be rendered incapable of going to school or child care, and if a baby-sitter is involved, she will have been rendered unconscious by aforementioned natural disaster.

Let me illustrate. My husband's job offers him far more opportunity to travel than mine, but he limits the number of trips he accepts and the number of nights he's away. He recently was away on business while I had a class to teach and a book deadline, but it was for only one night and only an hour from home, so how bad could that be? I probably even said as much out loud, which only taunts the Laws to manifest their might.

He'd left that morning before dawn. My getting three children dressed, fed, civil—or at least nonviolent—and finally in possession of backpacks and diaper bag: not a problem. Everyone arrived at school and preschool within the realms of On Time. My Supermom cape was fluttering in the breeze beside my laptop.

I was teaching a university class two evenings a week, during which my husband normally arrives home early from his job so I can leave in an unhurried manner for mine. With him out of town, I'd hired a competent baby-sitter—though admittedly, she'd never sat for us before, and Jasmine dislikes new sitters until they're properly broken in.

Still, the sitter arrived on time.

So did the tornadoes.

They were sighted a few miles from my house. We were being pummeled by rain and high winds and hail.

The only room in my house without windows is a tiny bathroom in the center of the downstairs. A sufficient tornado shelter—so long as the whole family doesn't need saving. The commode and sink and a tacky little lighthouse stool leave little floor space. Still, I billeted the three children inside with mounds of sleeping bags and pillows and snacks normally saved for special occasions. I pawed through drawers for candles and matches and batteries. The dog wanted in, of course, and the cats, frightened to the point of near-canine devotion, wanted to be on our laps.

Then the electricity went out.

I knew the chances of our house or car being hit by a tornado or by flying debris were quite small. But the television announcers—before the electricity popped off—had been asking cars to stay off the road.

And I could also see—by candlelight—the fear on the face of my oldest child, the one normally so confident.

I could hear the brave but higher tenor to the baby-sitter's voice: *Where again were the candles, the matches, the blanketsbatteriessnacks…?*

The crashing outside egged on the pounding, and the pounding only encouraged the moan of the wind.

I canceled class.

The baby-sitter stayed on for safety reasons and curled up with a flashlight to study for her anatomy test.

By candlelight and by feel, I fumbled to extract the dead batteries in my daughter's radio. The new ones I probably crammed in too hard. But the thing worked well enough to hear news of the latest funnel-cloud sightings.

At a break in the storms, the baby-sitter drove back to campus, and all three children begged to sleep in my room. The dog, with the unflappable cheeriness of all golden retrievers, suffers from a mortal fear of thunderstorms; she begged to share my bedroom as well. She's not typically allowed on the carpet, so I laid blankets on the floor beside my own floor pallet, put the big kids in my bed, and put the baby in her crib a few feet away. Eighty pounds of gold fur spent the night trying to crawl onto and not just beside me.

And Jasmine, who never gets sick, got sick.

Because, of course, of the Laws of the Traveling Spouse.

I was up repeatedly with her during the night.

At some point past midnight, just as I'd drifted back to sleep, the batteries I'd crammed into my daughter's radio exploded. Quite loudly. Scaring me clear up off my pallet and onto the dog, who was still trying to crawl onto me. Battery acid had leaked all over the counter.

I surrendered to having no sleep and decided to work.

But I'd forgotten that I'd given my laptop to the kids to watch DVDs in their half-bath-turned-tornado-shelter, and in the absence of electricity, we'd run the battery dead.

So I thought I'd knock out some grading—but having not held class that night, I'd not collected my students' papers.

I cuddled back up with the trembling dog.

Then, sometime in the wee hours, our power was, of course, restored, bringing the television blaring back on and lights everywhere.

My husband was going to pay dearly for this.

Which brings us to...

Law of the Traveling Spouse #3

Upon returning home, the Traveling Spouse is obligated to relieve Guarding the Home Front Spouse in any way he or she desires, particularly if Traveling Spouse (a) was bumped into first class, (b) was treated to fine ethnic cuisine at any time, (c) stayed in a hotel rated more than three stars, or (d) had free time while away to tour a museum or celebrated landmark, go to a sporting event, or (and this would be serious) attend a Broadway show. Eating crepes within view of the Eiffel Tower while on business, for example, puts you in very, *very* deep debt to your life mate, who is even at that moment toasting frozen waffles while dressing for work while feeding the dog while brushing the oldest child's hair while the middle child topples the syrup while the dog licks the syrup from the just-washed hair of the youngest.

Which brings us back to Law #3: that it might be wiser to forgo some of those trips or take the whole family along.

Actor Bruce Kuhn transatlantic commutes for his work while his wife, a painter, stays at home in Holland.

"My work is mostly on the road," he'll explain after insisting that you asked to see recent pictures of his two kids. "So when I'm home in Holland, Hetty gets whatever she needs—four, five hours a day when the sun shines, which is about four months of the year in Holland. I'll say, 'You want the morning or the afternoon?' 'Depends,' she'll tell me. 'Because if the light shines here, I'll work on this canvas, but if the light shines this way, I need to go work on that one...' She paints outdoors, from the light that hits her eyes, not from photographs."

He adds this last proudly, then says again, in case you missed it: "When I'm home in Holland, Hetty gets whatever she wants." Law #3 in action.

Law of the Traveling Spouse #4

The reality is, both spouses may need to limit traveling for a time or take the family along on business, if possible. I know such simple words don't capture the sacrifice they might imply. Decreasing travel can be one of the most difficult parts of a slowing-down season or a change in career. But if you're changing other parts of your three-career marriage and it still is just not working, you might need to look at how travel is affecting your marriage and your kids.

We've found that limiting the number of days away decreases the tendency for us to shift into what I think of as One Captain mode: having just Mommy or just Daddy in charge of the household. One broadcast journalist I interviewed admitted that after months of intensive travel, she was home during a particularly sticky sibling dispute, which her husband was handling. When she began intervening, he informed her, in so many words, that because of her absence, she'd ceded her right to handle this spat. She was stunned—and hurt. She was also inclined to agree that, in this case, maybe her husband was right. Maybe some things needed to change in her schedule and in their family dynamics.

In cases where one parent's profession requires a great deal of time away, the family must come up with ways of working together that don't permanently shut down the authority or input of the absent parent when that parent returns. But it can be tough, such families will tell you. It requires time to adjust and agreed-upon rules, like scuba divers resurfacing slowly to avoid the bends.

The Truth About Traveling on Business—and Giving It Up

Traveling on business was something I once approached with giddy excitement—at least about three months out when the travel agent was making the arrangements.

I dreamt of how many eight-hundred-page novels I could consume on the plane as I sat with a Diet Coke and pretzels all by myself, my seatmate and I happily ignoring each other. But now that I have children, who are way too much fun, by the week before the trip my excitement has turned to dread. By the evening before I leave, I am convinced that my family cannot survive without me and that I will be committing maternal abandonment, even for a couple of days, by crossing the tarmac and leaving my treasures with the person who fathers them.

On any return flight from a professional trip to home, I'm a mess, and my psychosis grows along with any time left sitting on the tarmac, my family at the other end of the flight. I've often misjudged my literary ambition on these trips, and rather than bring what my students inform me is never assigned by English professors, I dutifully tote along some Approved Reading, as if some Great Texts Reading Committee will be checking my book bag at the gate for something written by an author who appears on the Barnes & Noble café mural. I actually like these kinds of books, which I understand is a sign of acute strangeness. But when I travel on business, I miss my family too much to focus, and I squirm. I read the first fifteen pages and then begin peering across my seatmate's elbow to share her open copy of Grisham.

And so I love being home with my kids, and I miss them desperately when I'm away. But when a certain season of life involves my traveling for work very rarely or never, I miss business travel. A lot. The sense of independence. The validation of one's professional identity. The maid service and the mints on the pillow.

My friend Elisa, the editor whose unflagging work helped craft this book—she's also a mother—tags giving up business travel, the independence and sense of professional identity that comes with it, as one of the hardest challenges in choosing to become a stay-at-home parent or begin working from home.

Weekends away for Just the Girls can help in the independence department, as my friend Kay, now the director of fine arts for a private school, found during the years she was home with her son.

Or, if finances allow, staying active in one's professional organizations and attending its meetings can at least keep you connected—and sane, as my sister-in-law, a chaplain, did during her stay-at-home years.

But there's no easy way around the fact that it will be a loss. And for some of us, a big one.

Even as I tap away at this chapter, my husband is in DC at a conference where he'll be hearing some stars on the national political scene. Am I jealous? Oh, *yeah*. For me, there's no expense account tonight to pay for a meal, not even an unexotic, fast-food one. But I'm using this time, undistracted by chatting and laughing with him late at night, to finish a book. And he's cutting his trip far shorter than he'd have liked—even missing two of the key plenary speakers—to be back in time to pick up his end of the parenting rope while I meet a deadline. He volunteered this, and I accepted.

Someday we both might be taking advantage of more opportunities to travel on business. Someday—who knows?—I might travel more and he a bit less. Someday, I'm told, our children might grow a bit older. Meanwhile, the three-career marriage demands that everyone adjusts to the needs of the whole.

Now, for those whose marriages include one profession demanding truly frequent travel, the Traveling Spouse may need to exhibit abundant support for the Home Front Spouse, including:

1. Compensatory child care whenever possible, ideally involving sole cleanup of a diaper's volcanic eruptions
2. Explicit verbal acknowledgment of Home Front Spouse's sacrifices
3. Absolutely no carping over visible evidence of restaurant takeout or delivery
4. And, in extreme cases, material bribes

Truly, both spouses *must* discuss regularly and honestly who needs to give and who needs to get, and just what and how much, *in this season* to keep the whole crew afloat. And also what the next season might hold.

For the Doubters of Traveling-Spouse Theory

For doubters of these laws, may I suggest a simple experiment:

1. Take two working parents, both of whom face at least mildly urgent deadlines or meetings.
2. Add one, preferably more, offspring of at least average energy levels.
3. Have one parent kiss the other at the front door or on the tarmac of the airport.

4. Record the results of the following twenty-four to seventy-two hours. Weekends and work holidays do not meet the minimum stress requirements for proper completion of the experiment—unless the Home Front Spouse must work these days: ministers, doctors on call, newspaper delivery personnel...

5. Stir gently.

6. Stand back. And brace yourself.

Letting Go That Whale of a Goal

You Can't Do It All at the Same Time

C an you name this novel if I quote the first line?

"Call me Ishmael."

Think large international coffee chain. You stopped there this morning because it was more important that you be actually conscious at your first scheduled event of the day than that you be technically on time.

And Starbucks reminds us of... Exactly. Herman Melville's *Moby-Dick,* whose plot follows Captain Ahab, so obsessed with catching the white whale that he's unable to see when it's time to give up the chase for the sake of his crew and himself.

Our final glimpse of the captain is his being yanked underwater, a harpoon rope wound around his neck. Starbuck, the first mate, goes down with the ship— which would seem an unlikely image for a café chain, but clearly they're doing fine without input from you and me.

Ahab's a grisly reminder of what happens to any of us when we fail to figure out when it's time to let go of a particular focus or drive: the crash of our own ship. General destruction of Steven Spielberg proportions—in surround sound. And floating debris.

What follows is a list of some areas of life that many two-career couples with kids find they must let go of, at least for a time. You could probably add more and take some away, but here are some possible ways to help you and your crew keep your heads above water.

Letting Go of Specific Professional Goals or Ambitions

As you know from previous chapters, for former print journalist Vashti Murphy McKenzie, former Broadway actor Bruce Kuhn, former CNN anchor Andria Hall, and former ABC News religion correspondent Peggy Wehmeyer, letting go for the sake of family meant being willing to shift their ideas about where their career paths were headed. This didn't mean their careers were over or even necessarily stunted. In fact, letting go of one thing can be the beginning of something new and better. Realistically, it can also mean feelings of loss for which we ought to be prepared to face and balance with the good that's been gained.

When I last spoke with Peggy, now a full-time World Vision spokesperson, she was preparing to put her youngest child on a plane for college. She and her husband were becoming empty nesters, an often wrenching letting-go process itself.

Reflecting on her own experience of navigating kids and career, she said:

> You have to grieve those dreams you can't pursue, what you lose, and be grateful for what you have. Demanding to have it all is what children do. Being a mom and being a professional are both callings, but you have to know ahead of time where your first calling is. You can't wait until they collide.

As her life and her commitment to her own family demonstrate, at some point all parents must give up something—or lots of somethings—in their professional lives. But, she added, "Only *grieving* what you've given up makes you cynical and negative; only being *grateful* means you're in denial. You have to grieve *and* be grateful and hold those in tension."

Todd and I recently had dinner with new friends here in Nashville, Nonye and Anthony Ejiofor. The Ejiofors are originally from Nigeria, though they've lived in the United States for more than a decade. Their oldest child is the same age as my oldest, and their two younger, like my third, are adopted. All three of their children are good looking in the same way as their parents, handsome and regal. Nonye in particular carries herself like a woman who has never been flustered or daunted, never met a person she could not greet warmly or a job she could not master in a matter of moments. Whenever I see her, it's all I can do not to find a ring on her hand I can kiss.

But the hours of her current position as a social worker, she told us over dinner, had been insane. She'd been coming home late night after late night. It became intolerable for her family, and she'd just given notice. She decided she would run the nonprofit organization she'd founded and start a small business and let that be her professional focus. A huge shift, and not one without sacrifice. But Nonye knew when to let go. And when to direct her professional energies in ways that better fit with her family.

For novelist and short-story writer Doris Betts, having children and teaching and writing meant giving up "lots: other academic jobs, residencies, long absences [from home]." She told me:

> Early on, I did a certain number of writers' conferences that required my husband to be more of a hands-on father than *he* probably felt "called" to be. We could not have afforded live-in nannies, etc. But we'd both grown up in households where family took precedence, so these demands did not seem like a novelty. And, of course, to be a parent means that you can't always travel, do book tours and self-promotion, spend a semester here and another one there, trot up to the Library of Congress for a week of research, etc. The trade-offs are inevitable.

For some professionals who are parents, letting go means that the promotion to the upper reaches might have to wait for a season. For others, the goals to put on hold might not be self-promoting at all—and yet they still don't fit with the season of the family.

Racial reconciliation and urban-development activist Kathy Dudley once ran a shelter for recovering drug addicts and prostitutes out of her own house. Having grown up in poverty herself, the twelfth child of a sharecropper's family in south-west Virginia, she spent her young married life asking, "How can I help other people who are struggling with similar things as I did growing up?... I would find bums, prostitutes, usually at the doughnut shop because I love doughnuts, or the mall, and I would just bring them home because they had nowhere to go."

After beginning a family, though, it became clear to Dudley and her husband that her ministry focus needed to shift. For Dudley, being willing to let go for a time meant realizing that while her children were young, they needed a safer, more settled environment. So beginning with nothing but a soccer ball, a Bible, and the Dudleys' meager savings, she founded Voice of Hope Ministries in a low-income sector of west Dallas. The ministry that grew out of her being willing to close down and retool her original vision has resulted in hundreds of thousands of dollars of housing and scores of mentored and tutored youth who, through Promise Kids Club, have not only *not* dropped out of high school but have gone on to college and good jobs and excelled.

Sometimes we can't see the benefit of letting go until after we've made a diffi-cult change. From what we were certain were ashes, and only ashes, God can bring beauty; from what we thought was pure loss, God can bring the gain we'd never predicted.

Letting Go of the Notion That Parents Have Only Two Professional Choices

We often unwittingly base decisions on the only two choices we assume we have: (1) for husband and wife both to work two sets of long, full-time hours, or (2) for one of those people to resign and stay home full time until all offspring trot off into the world. For many of us, there truly are other options, *if* we're able to be creative or accept less income or demand less prestige or maybe take some profes-sional risks, perhaps even shifting careers for a time.

The numbers vary according to the sources one reads, but all sources agree that, compared to even ten years ago, more employers offer more flex time and part time and telecommuting and extended maternity/paternity alternatives to their employees than ever before. And the more of us out there looking for creative solutions, the more workplaces will be willing to listen. For those who choose to opt out of the outside work force for a time, a more flexible professional world would, ideally, be that much more likely to welcome us back. There's power, you know, in numbers. And in bullheaded perseverance.

In a telephone conversation, Secretary of Labor Elaine Chao told me how women entering the work force in such great numbers had been the catalyst for positive change, so that "the concern with balance between work and family has taken on paramount importance" and has become "a key public-policy issue." Employers are now learning, she said, that they "need to accommodate workers who have other priorities; that if a worker wants to leave the work force to come back at a later time, that ought to be possible."

So as you look at the options in front of you, practice some wild thinking. Maybe you *could* live on less, maybe the boss *will* be agreeable, maybe you *would* find more than enough clients working on your own. You may not decide to go the most creative or the most risky route, but shifting your perspective will give you a greater sense of freedom—and maybe the courage to try something out of the ordinary.

Letting Go of the Idea That You Can Do It All by Yourself

The seventeenth-century poet and Anglican priest John Donne is great fun to teach, partly because he startles my students with his frank allusions to sex. They're particularly astounded when, after Donne's conversion and his ordination to the Anglican Church and his becoming a devoted husband and dad, he *continues* his interest in sex. ("But now he's *married*," they protest.)

Donne also wrote—as you of course know but, because it's been a long day, have forgotten—that wonderful line, "No man is an island."

And for our purposes here, I don't think our friend the poet would mind our substituting *woman* where needed.

You were not created as an entity unto yourself.

A journey of mature faith is the opposite of what we learn in psychology classes: not a journey from dependence to autonomy, but in many ways the reverse—from thinking of ourselves as independent to recognizing our interdependency on one another and our absolute dependence on God.

So display your newfound maturity by being willing to accept help.

Even as I write this, my mother is roaming my house, in town for a visit because she remembered I had another book deadline approaching. With anyone else, this would be too hard on my pride—my family insists they will etch "I Can Do It Myself" on my tombstone. But accepting assistance from my own mother is something I can do and be kiss-the-feet grateful for it. Her timing is impeccable, never waiting for a wail for help, which will never come, but simply seeing long days and short nights out ahead and asking if this might not be a good time for her to do a little extra cooking and cleaning and tucking in.

We haven't always lived this close to my parents, and I value the privilege of having her nearby as a gift. I'd recommend her to you for invaluable help in your own life, except she's *my* mother. Stand back and leave her alone.

But for many of us, including me for most of my life as a mother, the any-time-you-need-it assistance of extended family is not an option.

My friend Lu, who's had several careers in her life, introduced me at her husband's seventieth birthday party to the baby-sitters, two sisters who'd helped care for her three children as the kids grew. Lu highlighted some of the best character traits of her daughter, Christy, also a friend, and attributed them to the sitters. Overhearing, Christy, who is my age, laughed, and agreed.

This has been a helpful reminder to my husband and me as we call sitters to fill in the gaps between his work schedule and mine. Our sitters include teens and college students who are remarkably talented in music, athletics, academics—young people who play hide-and-seek with my kids when I probably would not, who teach them guitar chords I've probably forgotten, who show them a great grip on the bat when I can't. These are young adults who've just returned from Indonesia, where they helped with tsunami relief, or they're on their way to Ecuador, where they'll help construct homes, and they speak of how the people live there, while my kids listen, wide-eyed. Which is far more effective than my harping about their eating their carrots because there are children starving in Africa. When chosen carefully, and not overdoing the hours, good sitters can be enormous assets to our children's ways of seeing the world.

When it's difficult or financially unrealistic to get this kind of extra help, consider trading baby-sitting duties with a friend or neighbor who has kids. Many churches have Parents' Day Out programs at minimal cost. Again, be as creative as possible. You're not copping out on parenting; you're trying to make your family work in the best way possible. Not only can we not do it alone, but calling in reinforcements can enrich our kids' lives.

Letting Go of the Aura of Being Cool

The truth is, I never was cool, not even at sixteen. I've only ever owned a total of two eight-track tapes; one of those was broken and the other was John Denver. But since having children, I've sunk to the Even Less Cool: a bulging diaper bag dangling from one shoulder, a laptop on the other. And now, since the purchase of the minivan that the third child made obligatory, I'm hopeless.

"Capitulation Mobile" is what a friend of mine dubs minivans. So very apt. I slide on my shades and skim my fingers across the radio buttons and toss back my hair like the woman beside me at the light this morning in her Mercedes convertible—but it just doesn't work for me anymore. My vehicle is blue, like hers, my hair long and blond, like hers, and I've rolled down my windows—the only two you can in a van—to get the same spring-air-in-my-hair effect, but it's no good. The Capitulation Mobile, ankle deep in soccer balls and Happy Meal toys and juice boxes and the whole family's books—we're a traveling library—labels me as a Mother of Multiple Children. The black business suit bought on clearance at Sears pegs me as a professional but one who's unclear where cool people shop.

Coolness is not within reach.

Perhaps minivans are even more of a plunge into Deep Dweebiness for fathers than for mothers. Tom and Ray Magliozzi of the weekend National Public Radio show *Car Talk* often observe that minivans, while very nearly mandatory for larger families who prefer to steer clear of gas-guzzling SUVs, could challenge a man's masculinity. Tom once announced that he'd neutered the family tomcat just by tossing it in a minivan and driving around the block.

It's best, I'm discovering, to admit who I am as a parent-professional and who we are as a family and face facts: by a factor of several thousand, I will listen to more VeggieTales Silly Songs in my car—okay, my *van*—than the Black Eyed Peas—and I had to call my friend Ginger just now to tell me the name of a with-it group to give as an example. Someday I may know who's the most recent winner of the most recent reality TV show, but right now I need to take any energy spent worrying about what I'm missing and use it to enjoy what I have—Bob the Tomato and all.

Letting Go of a Vibrant Social Life

I once read about the naming of the new female chief executive of a major publishing house that had never hired a woman in that post before. While her colleagues referred to her as extremely hard-working, they also implied she kept a bit more to herself compared to previous holders of her post. She apparently limited her nighttime social events—very important to her profession—to no more than three or four nights a week while her children were young. Despite her having a nanny, she felt it was important to put her own children to bed.

While three or four nights away might seem like too many to some of us, the point is a good one. If you have a number of social or professional acquaintances who have no children or have grown children, you may seem the dull, homebody bore. But you are in a particular season of life, and something's got to give—you may need to let a colleague sit down to a formal dinner for twelve while you read *Goodnight Moon* just one more time.

Before we had children, and even when we had just one, my husband and I used to give huge parties. Not lavish affairs or even remotely elegant. But now that our family has grown to the size and decibel level of one ready-made party, we have a grand total of two Christmas open houses a year and one Derby party—it's a horse race, not a party for hats. And we host steady streams of sleepover guests, for whom we pitch tents in the backyard, roast marshmallows, and practice our flapjacking in the morning (it's all in the wrist). Other than that, if you show up for dinner, you must carry in your own takeout, and we'll gladly clear off a place at the table.

I sometimes miss the mass gatherings—and I do still love a dinner out, when we don't spend half the meal under the table picking up crayons. But we're gathering friends who also have children as well as professional passions. These are people who can entertain toddlers with one hand and snap a pouting teen out of her funk with the other, all the while holding forth on the state of the nation and of their work. And these are people I want to know better. Those with grown children or no children sometimes still call us to meet for dinner—but they are the proud, the few, the godparents, who know they might be asked to change a diaper before dessert.

Letting Go of One or Two High Expectations

Paul Bothwell, a dear friend from Boston days, would be amused and a little appalled to know how often we quote him at our house. One of my favorite one-liners of his serves as good therapy. With four daughters and his and his wife's active involvement in professions, their church, and their community, Paul's stock answer to the awed "How do you do it?" question is this: "I just try to make the least of every opportunity." Type this out and post it over your computer screen, and the world will seem a brighter and more merciful place.

Truly, there's wisdom in being willing to let go of being a perfectionist in every area of our lives. Jimmy Carter is my favorite of all living American presidents, but I don't keep his bestseller *Why Not the Best?* on my shelf, since my answer for this season of life is *Because I'm So Blasted Tired.*

The thing is, we can't let "the best" get defined too broadly or defined by someone else for us. Yes, excellence has to be the goal if we take seriously parenting and using our God-given gifts. But "the best" doesn't have to apply to the sheen of the hardwood floors, where my dog—*well, isn't that lovely*—just tracked muddy ice in big smeary circles. "The best" doesn't have to include the state of my wardrobe and whether my belt always matches my shoes and whether my shoes are this season's fashion—I can assure you, they're not.

In the midst of all we manage, it's natural to feel you're failing sometimes. It's also natural, in the scurry of each day, to forget what is most important. But somewhere you've got to give yourself a break. That might mean going to bed even though the living room is knee deep in clean but only half-folded clothes, or letting someone else give the presentation this time, or serving the same thing for dinner three nights in a row. (My friend Linda Livingstone, the dean of a business school and a mom, suggests we all turn our kitchens into drive-through windows, where the delivery person pulls up.)

Letting go of perfection in some areas frees us to focus on excellence in those areas that truly matter: our spiritual lives, our family relationships, and the ability to take seriously the fact that we have been given good work to do.

Letting Go of the Notion That All Your Kids' School Projects Are All About You

I don't think of myself as competitive. So I don't know who that woman is who sometimes has so much to say when my older daughter walks in with a 91 percent on a math test.

"Would it have been *so* hard to check your answers one more time?" that woman who looks just like me would demand every time if I let her.

This is the same person whose hands nearly shake with the urge to tweak her son's art projects for him. The truth is, her son is already a more gifted artist than she is, but she knows the other mommies and daddies will be tweaking their children's projects tonight, and the lineup of talent in the hallway tomorrow will be stunning—some of the efforts barely touched by the children themselves. This woman knows that the competition is fierce out there—in kindergarten and throughout life—and she wants her children to win.

I, on the other hand, am more spiritually and emotionally enlightened than that woman who looks just like me and insists on using my name. *I* would rather my kids develop fine character and generous spirits and kind hearts.

Perhaps especially for moms, our children's performance—artistically, athletically, academically—can often be what sends us running for our Working Versus Stay-at-Home battlefield positions, to use the language of the Mommy Wars. As a writer, I'm probably perceived as being on both sides of the battle, or neither, a kind of Switzerland without the good watches and cheese. In this area, though, I often feel not only *not* neutral, I feel myself in danger of going to war with…myself.

It's as if I take on all the working moms' angst that we must prove *We have just plenty of time to help our children excel, and by they way, they're learning to be independent, too,* right along with the stay-at-home moms' concerns that we justify this time out of the workplace by showing *Our children are more stable and capable for our spending more time at their sides.*

And sometimes I want to scream at anyone who will listen, but most especially myself, that a cease-fire would be nice. That this is not all about me. Or, come to think of it, you. And that maybe one of us, starting with that woman who uses my name, ought to *let go* just a little.

Letting Go of the Need for Clarity

Some days it's okay just to do what needs to be done—bathe the baby who needs bathing, pay the bills that need paying, hand in the budget for work that needs handing in, listen to the teenager who needs you to curl up next to her in bed— and find delight in that duty. Some days we may not feel we're even a remote part of some grand, world-changing plan. So we perform the small good that we can, and we keep moving forward. And some days even stumbling forward ought to count as at least moving in the right general direction.

The ethicist John Kavanaugh, searching for direction in his own life, traveled to Calcutta to work with Mother Teresa among the sick, destitute, and dying.

> On the first morning there, he met Mother Teresa. She asked, "And what can I do for you?" Kavanaugh asked her to pray for him. "What do you want me to pray for?" she asked. He voiced the request that he had borne thousands of miles from the United States, "Pray that I may have clarity." She said firmly, "No, I will not do that." When he asked her why, she said, "Clarity is the last thing you are clinging to and must let go of." When Kavanaugh commented that *she* always seemed to have the clarity he longed for, she laughed and said, "I have never had clarity; what I have always had is trust. So I pray that you trust God."[1]

Yes, it's vital to dream and plan and be aware of where you are headed professionally and as a family. It is also vital to sleep. So if you don't have a sense of the grand plan today, maybe that's okay. Maybe that's a part of trusting in a God who holds the future and knows our hopes even better than we do.

Letting Go of the Portrait-Perfect-at-All-Times Family

No matter how much I want my personal and professional lives to run smoothly at all times, a well-oiled machine that others gather to watch with reverence and awe, I am realizing that this will not always, or ever, be true. At some point in the week, I'm going be late in getting papers graded, forget to back up my entire book manuscript, and run out of time for the grocery store, though I'd assured my spouse it was my turn and *of course, dear,* I knew we'd run out of milk. It's also likely that one of my children will belch loudly during a liturgical prayer—which I'm told leads directly to torching public buildings.

During the period that we were being examined by a social worker to be approved—or not—for adopting a child, our middle child, Justin, came into his own. His own *what,* I'm not sure. But it was an interesting several months for our formerly shy, sweet-spirited boy, by then a boisterous four years old.

The pressure was on, we all felt, to appear to be a family without flaw.

Here's how we fared:

When the social worker first came to meet us, he asked to interview each of the older children alone. Julia, though uncoached by my husband or me for this event, has been savvy from birth about What Adults Want to Hear. We could hear her showing the social worker around her room. "You see here," she was explaining, "I have probably a couple of hundred books. We love to *read* in this family."

"I see. What else do you do?" the social worker wanted to know.

"Oh," she said, speaking slowly so he could write down every word, "mostly just *read.* Mostly *classics,* you know. *Very rarely* television. Only about, I'd say, thirty minutes a week, and then only *informative* and *educational* programs."

Justin, meanwhile, was taking a nap.

Those of us playing the part of supremely calm and loving parents held our breath.

Maybe, we prayed, he wouldn't wake up in time.

He woke up.

In quite a state. He'd napped too long and was working up a good rage for the playing outside that he'd missed.

Just as the social worker was turning to leave Julia's bedroom, Justin stomped in. Justin had, without asking any supremely calm and loving parents, slipped on before nap an infant-sized T-shirt that Julia and I had tie-dyed for him when he was just one—so it was stretched and tearing across his chest. For pants, he'd pulled on to his legs a green turtleneck, the neck itself hanging between his legs.

His blond curls were tousled and tangled from sleep. A ringleted Hulk, he scowled up at the social worker, who reached for his notebook.

And shortly thereafter...

Standing in front of the entire congregation, our family was asked by our pastor what made each of us tick, what made "our hearts sing." Julia replied, "Reading." My answer was "writing." Todd's was "the people you see up here beside me" (for which he rightly received an entire congregation's adoring *awwwww*). Justin was given the microphone last. Our pastor repeated the question.

"Justin, what makes *your* heart sing?"

With very cool pukka shells around his neck, our gentle, cherubic five-year-old peered through dark, Blues Brothers shades at the congregation and said quite clearly into the mike, "Violence."

So there you have it.

And *still* we were allowed to adopt.

So surely your family, despite time crunches, despite crazy schedules, is at least—compared to ours—in pretty good shape.

And if you're still feeling uptight, perhaps it's time for letting go of the feeling that you ought never to feel uptight. So relax.

Letting Go of the Idea of Yourself as an Independent Operator

If you're Married with Children, you've already—like it or not—signed on to a team project. I recently heard my husband quoting to a young married couple from something he'd found true in his own life: one key to a good marriage is learning to shift one's thinking from "Is this good for me?" to "Is this good for my marriage?"

It's an important question to keep asking yourself when approaching career questions. You're a part of a crew, a working family, and for a family to work well, no one person can try to run things to personal advantage without regard for the others on board.

Letting Go That Hammer of Misplaced Guilt

Guilt, you know, is not always a bad thing. Like pain, it can be a warning, a signal to jump away from where your toes have sunk into hot coals. Guilt can be a sign that you've messed up and need to change the way you operate. In the area of analyzing kids and career and marriage and how we're dealing with these beautifully together, or not, guilt *can* be a sign, and a crucial one, that something's tilted way out of whack and needs correcting.

But.

But it can also be a burden we take on unnecessarily, a message we receive from outside forces and then carry about, hobbling as we go, and potentially, let it crush our vitality and our judgment. Physician and Stanford professor Jane Tan told me:

> Because I don't feel guilty about my choice [to work outside the home], the children never perceive guilt, and this is key. Children have an amazing alacrity for detecting conflict and guilt in their parents, and have no qualms about going for the kill. In fact, Andrew [her oldest] sometimes asks me why I have to go to work, that [some] other mothers stay at home to play with their kids. It was clear that he was testing my response. I told him that I love him, and that I enjoy being a doctor and that people depend on me. I enjoy this the same way that he enjoys other activities that do not involve my participation. Also, I noted that when I am happy, I have a lot more patience and I am more pleasant to be around. He was happy with this answer.

The key, then, would be to analyze what it is you're feeling, whether it's a cudgel crafted by someone else's expectations, which you're now wielding on your back, or whether it's a needed knock on the head toward a time for change. Dentist Jennifer Grant's summation of dealing with sadness or guilt on the kids-and-career front is simple and straightforward: "If it persists, do something about it. Change things. Life is too short to miss out."

Letting Go of the Idea That There'll Never Be Tensions—and That Tensions Are Bad

Well, *of course* there are tensions. It's a sure sign—along with that sharp shooting pain in your knee—that you're alive and kicking. Tension comes from one force pulling on another, and sometimes for you and for me, that's good pulling on good. Some days getting caught in the middle hurts, but the existence of tugs from two sides doesn't necessarily mean your life is all wrong.

Feeling tension might mean that you're blessed with a spouse with a spine, with a mind, with goals of his or her own, with kids who have talents, with a job that fills a calling or pays bills or maybe even does both. Tension might just be your reminder that this life you have is a privilege, so much good tugging at more good.

Of course some days we feel knocked clear off our feet. But next time you're feeling pulled, repeat this three times to yourself and see if it helps: *This tension I'm feeling today is a sign that I love and I'm loved, and that I'm incredibly lucky to be making a difference, both inside and outside the home.*

Okay, so repeating these words may not solve *all* your kids-and-career problems. But if it does, call me. We'll put the phrase on mouse pads and potholders and start our own business. Meanwhile, practice letting go of whatever's pulling *you* under the waves.

All Hands on Deck

Supporting and Celebrating One Another

I t seems to me that it's time we celebrated all the *good* of the working family, all we can learn from and affirm in one another.

Doris Betts's story has been an encouragement to me, a needed reminder that just as we watch and cheer on our children, our kids truly do see—or they will— in us parents more than just how well we fold their underwear.

Betts is an award-winning novelist and short-story writer. She raises Arabian horses, taught for years at UNC–Chapel Hill, and is a tough-minded, tender- hearted woman of faith. Though strong and independent, her marked southern drawl suggests magnolias and molasses. Several years ago, she was generous in let- ting me hammer her with the questions that were hammering me at the time about family, faith, and career.

"There's not a parent on the planet," she said,

whether working or stay-at-home, who doesn't feel guilt, at least regret, at being an imperfect parent. If it doesn't hit when the children are young and you're trying to decide whether to stay home from work because a child might be coming down with something, it's bound to come when they enter adolescence. Every rebellion then seems attributable to the cookies you…didn't bake.

I don't know when it comes for other women, but the time did come when my children were old enough to find my work as a writer made me as interesting as the neighborhood cookie expert.

Have We So Quickly Forgotten?

Much of the Mommy Wars discussion revolves around the negatives, gloom and doom on all sides—whether or not even part-time day care irreparably damages a child's emotional well-being or, conversely, whether children enrolled in preschool or top-flight day cares at an early age test at a higher level academically than their peers who stay at home. We hear that because more women work outside the home, the volunteer pools for Scouts and church and PTA are diminished. We read how so many families today eat too-fatty, too-salty takeout food for dinner—if they manage dinner together at all—rather than the chicken our great-grandmothers raised, wrung the necks of, plucked, and stewed themselves.

Have we forgotten that our great-grandparents were working alongside each other on the farm or running the little restaurant on the Lower East Side together? Nobody, not Mom and not Dad, had time to sit on the living room floor for a three-hour game of Chutes and Ladders. Everybody worked together, kids and parents, husbands and wives.

Historians point to the Industrial Revolution as the era that most radically divided the genders according to working "outside" the home. With a shift away from an agricultural society to increasing numbers of factory and office jobs, mothers remained in the home to care for young children.

And now, with the broad availability of telecommuting tools, more and more women and men are designing ways to recraft their family lives to allow for more time in sharing child-rearing. Too often we forget to celebrate not only a world of opportunity for women and girls, but also the chance for men to connect with their children in ways that simply can't happen when fathers only see their young for brief moments before bedtime. Yes, shared child-rearing means that men are expected to share in the mind-numbingly recurrent dirty work of soiled diapers and grimy kitchen counters and that women are expected to share in the stress and complexities of financial responsibilities and job evaluations. But this also means that both mothers and fathers share in the incomparable privilege of *being there* for their children's development and growth.

A New Perspective

It seems to me that there's not nearly enough said about the benefits to families as a whole when each member's gifts are recognized and supported. Just as we parents celebrate and stress over our kids' piano recitals, friendship difficulties, accelerated reader goals, soccer tournaments, and first proms, our children can grow in their understanding of the world, their faith, and how they might use their own talents when they understand something of their parents' work—including the professional gifts of a mom or dad whose outside-the-home working life is temporarily taking a different form.

We read a lot about stay-at-home moms versus working moms and how ugly the catfight has gotten, to the point of screaming matches on television talk shows. Why does this have to be a polarizing issue among women? How demeaning. And what a waste of time. Why aren't we helping one another navigate these waters, encouraging one another in that gutsy decision to launch a new career or to ask for that three-day week or to prove that working at home is more productive than in-office time or to insist on leaving the office at a reasonable hour?

And where are the daddies in this discussion? Many of these articles and books, *on both sides of the issue,* assume that somehow the dads' careers remain intact, unquestioned, unscathed, utterly unaffected no matter what the child care and career challenges. If we want to model for our children a partnership of mutual support, wouldn't our children find it fitting that Daddy might not be able to achieve all his career goals as soon as he'd like because he, like Mommy, is careful during these childhood years to limit the time he spends at the office?

Several years ago, Canada's only woman prime minister, Kim Campbell, made headlines when she insisted that parliamentary discussions cease each day in time for members to go home for dinner. Male members of Parliament commented quietly to the press how grateful they were for someone to have the courage to place boundaries on the workday, a gift to them all. And not surprisingly, they discovered they were much more productive in the time that they had, when no one was excessively hungry or tired.

Shouldn't this new century be a time less for Mommy Wars than for Two-Parent Peace Accords, moms and dads thinking creatively *together* about how to craft flexible solutions to care well and tenderly for their young and not permanently shelve anyone's gifts? Isn't it time we threw a few more streamers and confetti for the new era we're in and all the rich and wonderful things it means for our families?

The Sexiest Kind of Man

The first fall that Jasmine was home with us, I was teaching university classes in the evenings. Jasmine was still adjusting to the family and our recent moves, so Todd and I were intentional about limiting her outside child care. Todd sprinted home from his office two afternoons a week to tag team with me so I could go teach my class.

By the time I arrived home from teaching, his face was always glowing. "There's just something different," he'd gush, "about my being alone with the kids."

If I acted offended that my absence had been a plus, he'd hasten to paint flattering images: the monumental pull of Mommy, like the gravitational pull of the sun. But I try not to suggest this. First, because it's not necessarily true, and second, because I do know this: when my husband spends time with our kids, despite the inevitable discipline challenges every parent faces, he looks like a thirsty man with his pail being filled. And then he runs with it, sloshing.

Without my working at least some of my professional hours outside the home, I might never sufficiently get out of the way to let him connect with the kids as he's learned to and as the kids love. And that certain smile on his face when he's being a dad at his best—when he's tussling with our kids or hearing their hearts or showing he knows where the crib sheets are kept—is just so *very* attractive.

An ethics professor of mine once conducted this small experiment. We'd just finished reading Carol Gilligan's now-famous gender-difference study *In a Different Voice*. The first day of discussion, the professor had the men in the class circle their desks at the center of the room while the women, who were not allowed to speak, sat on the outside.

On the second day, we reversed it, the women circling our chairs in the center and addressing a number of controversial issues while the men, consigned to silence and the periphery, strained in their seats like big, rangy dogs on leashes.

The experiment did confirm a number of Gilligan's points about the relational versus the goal-orientated tendencies of the genders.

But just as memorable, somewhere in the second day's discussion, as the men looked on, gagged, choking on the words they couldn't say, a female student commented that one thing exciting to her about the shifting gender expectations in our society was that men were taking so much more responsibility with and interest in young children.

Other women quickly agreed.

"There's nothing more sexy," one woman sighed, "than a big strong guy holding a baby."

"Oh, YEAH!" was the general wistful, lusty—in all interesting senses of that word—response from the inner circle of women that day.

On the third day, half the class arrived carting baby dolls under their big, strong, modern-male arms.

Whoever said men don't listen well?

And it's true, you know. It's a new era for supporting and celebrating one another: mommies *and* daddies, parents and kids.

When You're Part of the Crew

Just before Julia turned two, my first book came out. The cover of the book, *Grit & Grace,* was purple with brightly colored dancing, praying, twirling figures—the cover artist really outdid himself, I must say, and Julia was fascinated with the design. Or maybe she understood us when we showed her where the book was dedicated to her and to my mother. At any rate, she became a one-girl publicity machine, toddling through Barnes & Noble stores all over New England and North Carolina, accosting strangers with "Buy Mommy's book!"

A preteen now, Julia asked the other day if she could be a medical doctor *and* write books *and* have kids. Come to think of it, she didn't ask as much as she assumed.

"Well," I answered, "maybe not all at the same time, but why not? So what kind of population would you serve as a doctor? Maybe a clinic for low-income families? Or maybe take medical trips to Sudan like Dr. White-Hammond?"

She cut her eyes slyly at me, already enjoying my reaction to her saying this: "Naw, I'd just see how much money I could make for myself. And buy one of those mansions like we just passed on our way home. And then I'd get myself…"

She's a part of our crew. She sees us when we're selfish with our time and our income and when we're not. So she knows all the wrong answers and just how to word them for full cringe effect.

This very week, Julia's on a mission trip to Appalachia, and the adult leader, Danielle, just called to ask a quick question. But while she had me on the phone, Danielle chuckled, she wanted to report something I might like to know. In the process of the kids' building a wheelchair ramp for a woman who'd not left her house for five years, they'd chatted with the elderly couple and learned that sometimes the wife couldn't make her husband hear her from the other end of the house, small as it was, when she needed help. It was Julia who had the idea of buying the couple a baby monitor for the house and had now begun collecting money from all the kids.

Now frankly, Julia's good heart and generous spirit toward money just might come more from both sets of her grandparents than from her parents. The impatience, now *that* she gets from her father and me in a double, near-lethal, dose. But it's been my prayer that even as we've struggled, sometimes failing, to parent her well, God might use even our faults for good. So the report that she'd seen a situation she didn't like and impatiently wanted to do something about it gave me reason to hope.

Laboring Together

When Justin began day care, we faced a new set of crew-working-together challenges. He split a full-time slot with Sam, the son of my friend Amy, who was working full time but had flexible hours and whose husband, like mine, could share part of the care. I'd nursed Justin for thirteen months to fend off every creepy sickness-producing organism known to humankind, and weaned him when I did only because he was enormous, a blond gorilla dressed in Garanimals. He was fast approaching a size bigger than me, and people were beginning to stare when I carried him on my hip. But I didn't foresee the dreaded ear-tubes-at-the-wrong-angle challenge, which led to countless days he couldn't go to child care. Every week was a Rubik's Cube of scheduling.

I eventually came to the realization that I should teach on Tuesdays and Thursdays, since these were my husband's lightest days, and my grading and preparation could be done from my home office on his heavier days. This schedule allowed for all manner of childhood emergencies, colds, flu, and earaches. Before this enlightenment, though, there were times when my husband postponed crucial meetings and at least once when, rather than canceling class, I lectured on William Faulkner with my son draped over my shoulder. As it turns out, you really don't need two hands to write Yoknapatawpha County on the board.

When any of our kids have been genuinely ill, we have pretzeled our schedules to keep them home in bed, where chicken soup could be served and vaporizers could steam up windowpanes and small plastic animals could roam through the caves of the bedclothes. But on the merely feeling-fine-but-still-contagious days, a baby sling is a many-splendored thing. Consider this: in agricultural societies, children go to work with their parents, typically their mothers, every day. Strapped to their parents' backs or their fronts, the children learn both the necessity and the value of hard work, as well as their own worth, as they are close enough to feel the parental heartbeat and hear the parental breathing and pull the parental hair.

Just a few days ago, National Public Radio interviewed a young Indian woman whose parents had run a hotel where their family both worked and lived. She and her siblings, she recalled, grew up running ice to room 47 and blankets to room 228. The family eventually made enough money to buy a nice house in the suburbs. But in the suburbs, she added, she missed knowing she was playing a vital role in the family's survival and potential success.

My daughter Jasmine adores riding in her purple backpack, a gift from former neighbors in Texas. Possibly this is partly because we hike a good bit as a family, and she associates the backpack with pink rhododendrons and cavorting streams and grand panoramas of the Blue Ridge Mountains—or maybe she just likes the

gentle jolt of the ride. But she is happy, too, when from her perch she is oversee-
ing the loading of a truck with relief supplies for Hurricane Katrina victims. I pray
that maybe, somehow, those hours of watching will become a part of her as she
comes to the point of making choices herself.

Teenagers Watching and Throwing a Party

The author of *Ellen Foster* and other acclaimed novels, Kaye Gibbons writes gor-
geously and trenchantly of relations between parents and children. Not surprisingly, since the imagination draws material from reality, she is the mother of three
daughters, two of them teenagers. In Gibbons's living room, she describes, sits a
rolling cart holding all the books she and her daughters are currently reading. Day
in and day out, her daughters watch what it means to be passionate about one's
work, to truly love what one gets to do for a living—and that the best work is
about far more than money.

Also the mother of teenage girls, broadcast journalist Peggy Wehmeyer was
invited as a speaker and consultant to the university where I worked at the time.
When I met with her, she'd just come from a meeting with the university's top brass,
and she was still shaking her head as she recounted the story to me. She'd entered
the conference room smiling, nodding, shaking hands with the president, the
provost, the deans, the key decision makers of the university—all men. Only men.

"But where are the *girls*?" she demanded.

I love this frankness, the courage to call strikes as you see them. Where *are* the
girls at this table of power? Where are the people of color? During our downtown's
lovely gentrification, what will happen to the people who slept here every night on
the sidewalk? What are we doing for someone else with all God has given us? And
are we, as parents, asking these questions out loud in our homes?

Kids and teenagers don't miss a thing. Not when we speed through the school
zone, not when we spend too much time primping in the mirror—not any of the
ways we invest our time well or don't.

Having had a voice in and through ABC's nightly news has now given
Wehmeyer a voice as a spokesperson and radio host for World Vision, the largest
Christian international development and hunger-relief agency in the world. She

described to me how her daughters cheered their mother on as she began speaking to groups on behalf of World Vision and how they celebrate with her as her skills help educate and raise awareness in this country about the plight of the poor and oppressed.

The crew can learn together, and together they can throw a victory party.

Time Not Quite Alone

Having children means a willingness to surrender much of one's private time. Life becomes an affair of Over the Bounding Main—*together.* In parenting, captaining one's own day with no regard for others happens only for the irredeemably irresponsible and the out of town.

On the rare mornings when I'm creeping out to catch a predawn flight and I'm already desperately missing my children and would give three of my front teeth to have them spontaneously wake up and throw their arms around me—those are the mornings they sleep like angels on Valium. But on the mornings I am rising before dawn to write or to pray or better still, both, the chances of my crawling out of bed early enough so that I can creep to my office unheard are minimal—about the same likelihood our backyard sandbox is growing its own adjoining ocean. It doesn't matter how early it is. There can be a five or a—heaven help us—four in the hour's place on the digital clock. I can skip brushing my hair, since children can, apparently from another floor and at the other end of the house, detect sounds of the dead cell material that grows from my head making contact with nylon bristles. (All children, I firmly believe, are born with motion sensors and have them secretly removed by a private surgeon when they turn thirteen and begin sleeping until noon, utterly unperturbed by the roar of the Saturday morning vacuum beneath their beds.)

So I slip into my office and slide into my desk chair careful not to wake anyone with, say, too much breathing. Now, my office is separated from the foyer of our house not by sturdy, solid doors but by a translucent curtain that I pull when (a) I'm approaching a deadline and the office's wood floor has disappeared under pieces of helter-skeltered manuscript or (b) I'm working in the wee morning hours. All three children are now old enough to understand what the closed curtain means: Mommy is working and Daddy will have to find the Band-Aids this time.

Julia, now more young woman than child, moves with long legs much like a young racehorse, no foal's pitter-patter still left in her gait. She bursts through the curtain only when the swell of middle-school news simply cannot be quelled.

The two younger ones, though, approach softly only in the morning. Justin is in football pajama bottoms and a T-shirt that hangs to his knees; Jasmine is in a pink princess sleeper with treaded feet. They tiptoe to the edge of the curtains, then twirl themselves, silently, in the sheers.

"Good morning, guys," I whisper, less concerned with waking my husband than with scaring away whatever almost-thought hangs at the edge of my mind but hasn't yet made it to paper.

Justin speaks for them both: "We're not bothering you, Mommy."

"Yes, I can see that, sweetheart."

"But Mommy?"

"Yes, big guy?"

"We just came to say that we love you."

Which is the end of my writing alone that morning.

It's God's kindness, we're told, that leads us to repentance. And it's my kids' sweetness, they've learned, clever children, that leads me to lay down the laptop and hug them. And forget where I was in my writing and make breakfast instead.

The truth is that I do crave time alone to write every day. I find it emotionally, spiritually, and psychologically essential—and necessary to my being a somewhat cheerful, marginally reasonable, and occasionally contributing member of society. Ideally, "alone" means more than ten minutes of concentration uninterrupted by the morning choruses, *Mom, is there more clean Star Wars underwear?* and *Mom, can you brush my hair?* and *Mommmyyyyy!* from the baby, which means, variously, *Tell my brother to quit setting me down on my head* and *I need to pour more soy sauce on the dog's nose and I need to do it NOW.*

But letting our kids see what our working worlds look like teaches them irreplaceable lessons. Letting them know that sometimes we need to pull a curtain and be alone and sometimes we need to drop everything to make Mickey Mouse waffles gives them a sense of the value of work and the immeasurable value of family. The idea that work can serve others and that spouses can share each other's excitement is contagious to children—apparently, even at four in the morning.

The View from the Cleft of the Rock

Few of us would choose personal or professional turmoil, but one of the gifts of such times of transition is what our children can learn about character, values, and perseverance.

When I interviewed Diana Garland, a successful grant writer and dean of the School of Social Work at her university, she recalled the time years before when, as an issue of integrity, she chose to publicly denounce some recent decisions of the president of the educational institution for which she worked at the time. The night before she was to make her speech, she sat with a lawyer at the kitchen table and went over both her own contract and those of the faculty members for whom, as dean, she was responsible. She knew that not only would her words get her fired, they would also mean the beginning of the end for her colleagues. Her young son John was sitting on the steps of their home, she only learned weeks later, and was listening to the whole thing. "I worried," she said, "what kind of impact the coming family crisis would have on him."

Mothers aren't supposed to crow about their own children in interviews, and Diana didn't. But as the outside observer, I can: John Garland has become an adult deeply committed to issues of injustice, poverty, and hunger. You have to assume there's some link between the young man devoting his life to making the world a little more fair and a boy listening on the stairs to his parents bracing for the financial and emotional blow from the loss of a job due to a principled stand.

I'd already flipped off the tape recorder when Diana rose from her desk. "I've never been able to see way out ahead," she concluded as we walked to the door. "For me, God's call is like Moses hiding in that cleft of rock and only seeing God from the back, after God's passed by."

Yes. It's like that in raising children too, isn't it? You never know day to day what they're learning just by being part of the crew, what they're soaking in about career and marriage and what it means to listen—or not—to God.

Learning on the Road

We can find intriguing examples of families working together all around us, when we're paying attention.

Last week I spoke with Shannon Sedgwick Davis on the phone. She recounted the crisis that she, twenty weeks pregnant, and her husband, Sam, faced in Rwanda when she nearly lost the baby. Whole villages, she said, began praying for her. The archbishop of Rwanda became a particular friend and supporter in prayer. Little Connor William Davis survived and was given an additional middle name, Manzi, meaning "brave one" in Rwandan. Reflecting on the close involvement of her family with her work and the travel it entails, she named "significant exposure to the world" as one important gift she believed she and Sam were giving their son. They recently filed papers to adopt a Rwandan child.

Yesterday I'd arranged for what I'd billed in my own mind as a working lunch. I only wanted to hear this woman's story of balancing her singing career and her kids, then be on my way quickly with a handful of notes. What I found was a friend, the kind who snickers when you do, the kind who's currently reading what you've been meaning to buy. And I found over lunch another hopeful example of families working together.

Karla Worley had been a studio singer early in her career—crooning jingles from nine in the morning to nine at night was how she described it to me. And she's sung and toured with groups such as the Gaithers, on whose bus she carted her infant son once children began to appear in the picture. Her husband, Dennis, meanwhile, was a well-respected producer and A&R (Artist and Repertoire) guy for a number of record labels. When they decided that Karla should go on the road to perform as Karla Worley, no longer as anyone's backup, Dennis ditched his own career to be her manager and travel with her. Karla wrote a number of books along the way and spoke at conferences and seminars.

Their children are teenagers now, one college age, and several years ago they quit traveling.

"I'm one of those people the Lord just speaks pretty clearly to," Karla recalled. "And the Lord let me know it was time to come off the road."

But Dennis hadn't reached that point yet and couldn't see where the family income would come from.

"So I waited for him to know too," Karla said matter-of-factly.

Dennis knew, too, six months later. It was another year after that before the two could fill all the bookings to which they'd already committed. The future was anything but clear. And then, unsought—in fact, initially unwanted—came a job for Dennis in a field he'd never considered before and in which he now excels.

Karla glanced up from her tomato basil soup. "My husband," she informed me, "is a genius."

Having seen him at work, I was quick to agree.

It occurred to me later that I should ask Dennis for a similarly laudatory word for his wife. But then I realized he'd already said plenty of what he thought of her gifts: his willingness to walk away from his own career in order to support hers. It doesn't get more eloquent or heartfelt than that.

Meanwhile, their oldest son, Seth, the first of three boys, the baby who rode along on the bus with his mother on tour, has become an artist in his own right; he's now a budding filmmaker who's been given encouragement and support from the community of faith and artists around him. Maybe he breathed too many tour-bus fumes, or maybe it was the air of creativity and people thrilled to be doing what they loved—people who give and get strength from one another.

Life Is Good

Over the years, my own husband has cheered on my teaching and ministry and writing through seasons of breathtakingly low incomes and so many rejections, including one New York literary agent I'd never contacted but who sent a form letter anyhow—a kind of preemptive strike letting me know to get lost before I showed up. Yet, having every reason not to, Todd has supported the writing, the teaching, the ministry, and celebrates the good days in grand, big-gestured Italian style. And, thanks be to God, he has never once compared our paychecks.

I watch my children watching that.

We've also learned that with some creative thinking and the assistance of modern technology, we can often combine business travel with family. Even as I tap this out, I'm rolling along in the passenger seat of our blue Kia van, no frills, and watching my laptop battery drop dangerously low. I'm getting a bit of work done en route from Chicago, where Todd had business. I'm calling this, for the moment, alone time, since two of the three children have miraculously dropped off to sleep and the third is happily putting Cheez-It crackers between each of her toes—

which, when you're not quite two, takes a good deal of concentration. I'm reminded that not all professions could operate in a rolling blue Kia with one hand on a keyboard while the other hand supplies a toddler with further cheddar toe-toys. Surgery, for instance, would be difficult here. As I write, my husband is providing a running commentary of his thought life, which currently seems to be focused exclusively on finding the Starbucks he was just sure he'd seen at this point on the way up. He is determined, he lets me know, not to stop to change the baby's diaper until he has found his Holy Java Grail. But we're just outside the greater Paducah, Kentucky, not-so-metropolitan area and have just passed Joe Bob's Flower Farm—truly its name—with not so much as indoor plumbing in sight. It's clear to me that the baby will be swimming in overflow leakage by the time we find the next Starbucks.

To amuse herself, the toe-accessory Cheez-Its having ceased to please, the two-year-old has begun pulling the hair of the sleeping six-year-old, and the ten-year-old wakes wanting to play Auto Bingo. All three are awake now, and I switch from my professional calling as a writer—which requires too much quiet—to my calling as a college professor. I once learned that Charles Dickens could compose his novels while sitting in his own drawing room full of guests. Perhaps so, but (a) the man was brilliant and (b) he died of exhaustion.

In any case, I need at some point to have read *Slaughterhouse Five* before I hold forth in class on its mysteries and virtues. Having read little of substance during my formative years, but having seen lots of really great football, I now make it a habit to assign books that I should have read in tenth grade.

So I settle for just reading and taking notes to prepare for a class. This way, I'm still able to help the older children in looking for the Auto Bingo–mandated silo—that's easy—and the police car they badly need for a full card. Julia has now chewed her mozzarella string cheese into the shape of a sword, and needs, understandably, her mother to applaud her artistry. I am vaguely aware, though, that some of my best thoughts as writer and as professor have become casualties of doling out rainbow Goldfish and juice boxes and attempting to hold a conversation with one side of my brain.

Finding that I don't actually have enough halves of my brain to read and listen and respond at the same time, I am moving from amusement to frustration, so it's time to insist on stopping the car—Starbucks or not—to change a diaper and switch drivers. I've not gotten as much work done on this trip as I'd hoped. But then, as my husband would gladly point out to you, I've never yet seen the day when I did get done what I'd hoped.

The point just now, though, is we're together. Learning. Reading. Eating. One of us snoring and now waking up with a start and a snort. I'm not naming names.

Todd comments on the urban ministers he met with in Chicago—what they're doing well and how that might be replicated in Nashville among university students there. The children eavesdrop and ask questions.

We're hearing the National Public Radio news. The Big People slip smiles to each other as the two oldest children rail in response to certain politicians' sleazy sound bites: "Can you *believe* this guy?" A bad habit they've picked up from their parents.

We're exchanging tidbits about school and work and friends and favorite books.

We're recalling the most spectacular of the Chicago skyscrapers—and can anyone remember the architects' names? Because I never can.

We're discussing what should be done for peace in Sudan and Iraq and biting mozzarella into merciless swords.

We're teaching and loving one another.

We're sticking Cheez-Its between our toes and feeling fine about that.

And life, together, is good.

Help for the Hopelessly Seasick

Some Tools for Survival

What follows is the remaining collection of valuable counsel and random tips that I've gathered in the process of interviewing wiser-than-I women and men for this book—and of learning a thing or two along the way myself, mostly by blowing it royally sometime in the past.

As with any advice on this subject, take what is helpful and toss out the rest—gleefully, please, and with no added guilt for goals you and your family have not yet achieved, or never intend to.

No doubt you could add your own superb survival suggestions to this chapter if you and I could meet for coffee. So maybe someday…

Receive Each Day as a Gift

It's tempting to wrap up this book with thoughts on the crucial issue for all of us: time and the screaming lack of it. But as I recently reread Dorothy Bass's book *Receiving the Day: Christian Practices for Opening the Gift of Time,* I was struck by her description of how we live "perpetually out of sync, when time is more problem than gift."[1]

"When time is more problem than gift" continues to flash through my days like the yellow caution signs of the winding mountain roads where I grew up. "When time is more problem than gift" reminds me of the moments I let my Day-Timer overwhelm my courage or distract me from the awe and the gratitude I can bring to the treasure that is this very day.

Dorothy Bass is one of those individuals whose feet seem more firmly planted than mine, her eyes more fully fixed, not glancing down at her watch, not peering through peripheral vision for the person she needs to catch next. She is a professor and a wife and a mother, so it's not that she's less busy than the rest of us. Perhaps she's just determined to let prayer tap out the beat of the day instead of the frantic pounding we all hear from the outside.

In *Receiving the Day,* Bass reminds us of morning prayer in the liturgical tradition, including "Open my lips, O God, and my mouth shall declare your praise," preparing us to enter the day with gratitude and to retool our tongues away from destructive tendencies. Drawing wisdom from the rhythms of Benedictine life and its "sanctification of time," she lines out ways to reclaim the day as belonging to God so that we may ready ourselves for bold, creative, and faithful living.[2]

We're all over-the-top, busy people. Agreed. But isn't there also a certain comfort in being so busy, reassurance of our deepest insecurities that we are *important* people, people whom other people are desperately trying to contact and invite to meetings and speak with before making decisions? Our busyness becomes our badge of honor, the flashing marquee of our smarts and our value. And we sigh that if only we had just an eighth day in the week, a twenty-fifth hour in the day... But the truth is that we'd fill that, too, to the point of still needing more, still feeling harried, still slamming against the end of the day breathless and hounded by what's been left undone *again.*

I was recently reminded of a poem by Jane Kenyon I read in graduate school. Written a few years before Kenyon's diagnosis and death from cancer, the poem speaks of the simple privileges of getting out of bed "on two strong legs," of eating a perfect peach, of taking the dog for a walk through a birch wood, of spending a morning doing "work I love," lying down with a life mate, eating dinner together. Along with these unremarkable watermarks of the day is the refrain "It might have been otherwise," washing into and over the poem, until a final, prescient, "But one day, I know / it will be otherwise."[3]

And indeed, for all of us, things will most assuredly one day be otherwise: the children, we pray, will become potty-trained and easier to take on cross-country road trips—but they will also one day launch into lives of their own. The loved ones who've given us life cannot, we're pained to see, always stand taller and stronger and lead the way. Our own bodies will one day betray the contract we thought we had with them. The careers we've so carefully trained for will flux and change with the seasons.

Time, we must learn, is a gift. And in receiving it as a gift, our sense of the day becomes radically reoriented. Stress will still be present. But even stress is just one component of the package: the duties and the delights.

So in the midst of navigating the full-sails run of family and work, to live with a trembling sense of gratitude for the day—in all its predictable mess and hurry—is *the* most important step toward finding not more time in the day but more meaning and fullness and joy in the time.

Establish a Rhythm of Prayer

My friend Milton Brasher-Cunningham, who is a writer and chef and minister and musician, wrote recently how aware he'd been lately of his own exhaustion, the over-the-top, harried state of his existence. And how everyone he met through his work echoed the same thing: "I'm so tired...so busy...so tired.

"If life has rhythm," Milton wrote, "I want to talk to the drummer."

Well said.

One way of reclaiming a rhythm to the day is to stake out a regular time—or times—for prayer. In the Christian liturgical tradition, prayer is an acknowledgment of the human need for regular, predictable spaces in the day to reconnect with God, to hear the lyric of a life that is not driven by iPods and the frantic ring of the phone. I know: you don't have time. Neither do I. And you were up late catching up with your spouse and cleaning the kitchen and checking the kids' folders for school and then the baby got up in the night and... Me too.

But I know the person I am when I'm wholly checked in with power and wisdom that doesn't come from my own inner deformities, and then I know the person who also claims to be me—the one you couldn't *pay* me to live with.

Beginning the day with prayer and letting it infuse all the rest of the hours gives perspective to the stresses and gusts ahead, gives purpose to all your mad dash and mine. It reminds us of who we are, what we have been, and where, just maybe, God is leading us next.

Dietrich Bonhoeffer's prayer life led him to the conviction that grace could be costly, which led him to join the resistance movement against Hitler. Before the war ended, Bonhoeffer was caught by the Nazis and executed. So this question he asks about prayer carries extra weight:

> Has it transported her for a few short moments into a spiritual ecstasy that vanishes when everyday life returns, or has it lodged the Word of God so soberly and so deeply in her heart that it holds and strengthens her all day, impelling her to active love, to obedience, to good works? Only the day can decide.[4]

Prayer can become something we crave—and can't live without.

Prayer can also become a part of your family's daily rhythm. As a family, try keeping a journal of prayer notes: the requests and the gratitude and the pleas for wisdom. Let your kids refer back to the requests and thanks there. I never cease to be humbled with the way my kids remember, unprompted, to pray not just for their own squabbles and struggles and hopes but also for specifics in their parents' professional lives and for children and families they've learned about, often through Todd's and my work. My kids remember well to speak to God of these things and my own spiritual and professional life takes note and learns from them.

Affirm Your Spouse

I love to hear people speak in glowing terms of their spouses, especially men who wax goofy about their wives' professional abilities. That's something new and improved we can paste across the labeling of this new era with pride. I just finished a meeting with a top university administrator who, in trying to make a certain point, slipped into a beautiful tangent on how his wife completely revamped the orchestral programs in the last place they'd lived. As I listened to him, I was caught up in his enthusiasm, his love for his wife, and his pride in what she'd achieved.

Affirmation—to your spouse's face *and* behind his or her back—is a wonderful way to help the three-career marriage work. Just as criticism breeds criticism, affirmation has a way of multiplying itself, and some is bound to find its way back to you. When you talk with your spouse, don't be afraid to offer specifics about what's going on in your own working world or what you're dreaming about for the future. If you're nagged by the feeling that your spouse cares little about your professional life, find a gentle but honest way of saying so.

You or your spouse may not have grown up with good role models on this, so be patient with each other. Remember that your kids are watching their parents' interactions and will mimic what they see—which means, potentially, yet more mutual encouragement bouncing about your home.

My husband does better on concrete forms of affirmation than I do, often coming home with articles he's found or books he's suggesting we buy relevant to my professional life. A plaque here, a great quote there that he took time to write down… To my credit, I've shown plenty of enthusiasm, thanks very much, for his professional gifts just by being willing to relocate all over the face of the earth and become close, personal friends with more real estate agents than I'd like to remember.

Consider Every Decision as Part of a Whole

This means that all job offers, all decisions for one person to go back to school, all opportunities for travel or relocations or promotions—which might entail more money but longer hours—have to be viewed *not just as one person's career* but as part of the whole family structure. The decision of whether one child should play soccer with a higher time-commitment travel team or with the YMCA league likewise must be made as part of the whole family rigging. One family member's increased medical needs will impact both parents' perspectives on their careers, with nobody's professional world off-limits for discussion. All pieces must work together or the whole thing comes flying apart.

Sit Down and Talk

In sorting through all the voices that tell us what we ought to do and be, it's easy for any of us to get blown off course. With a spouse who supports only one aspect of who you are—just your interest in work or just your devotion to kids, for example—you can certainly keep sailing ahead, but the winds aren't at your back. And the journey can begin feeling awfully lonely. Which can become dangerous waters for your marriage.

So sit down and talk, ideally on a regular basis. Compare visions of what each of you thinks family life ought to look like for this season and, as much as you can, make general plans for the seasons ahead. As in Sudoku, the puzzle-game craze, your task is to help make the variables all fit together: the emotional state of the kids at this age, the demands of each person's job, and the household cleanliness level and number of home-cooked meals each person thinks is ideal, to name just a few.

It's not that any of us has time for these talks; it's that we don't have time *not* to have them. Think of it as an investment, compounded daily. You can scrape together what time you need to invest now or be painfully, hair-rippingly sorry later.

One statistic on contemporary family life I read announced that the average couple with more than one child spends no more than five minutes a day discussing anything outside the mandatory life-business of who is picking up which child from which place. In reflecting on this to a friend with four children, I added that surely that number couldn't be right.

"No way," my friend agreed, "five minutes is much too high."

It was said half tongue in cheek, but he proceeded to insist that many days he and his wife struggle to find time for more than just MapQuesting the family's week. A good marriage can survive a short time of such traffic-pattern conversations. But over the long haul, without some heart-to-heart talks about what's going well and what's not, what you long to do but haven't yet, or what you see as your purpose in your life's work, your marriage won't stay as good as it could be.

Compare Mental Models

When our friend Paul in New England suffered a severe head injury, his cognitive therapist coached him on specific communication skills. He learned how to check to be sure that what he thought he heard was what others were actually saying and to map out on a dry-erase board how his way of thinking looked.

The question the therapist taught him to ask in group settings became a phrase we now use in our family, usually in friendly enough fashion, though every once in a while between clenched teeth: "So, then, what's *your* mental model of this?" It never ceases to nudge one of us to clarify what our expectations are—for ourselves, our spouse, our kids, and our rhythm of life. And how, perhaps, the family could work together to meet those expectations or how those expectations might need to shift.

Make Couple-Summit Meetings as Pleasant as Possible

The subject matter of navigating the three-career marriage can be difficult and delicate, especially if one spouse is resistant or unsupportive. So at least try to find pleasant settings and times of day—in other words, *not* as you're both standing over a hot stove and a toddler is practicing for a role in the *Animal House* food fight, and *not* late at night when someone (not you, of course) is already edgy and exhausted.

My husband and I find Tex-Mex nachos work well, a favorite baby-sitter at home with the kids. The kitchen table, after the children are snug in their beds, can also work, especially when both people's perspectives and ideas are helped on their way by two big bowls of Ben & Jerry's. (Don't try taking turns eating out of the carton this time—you have enough negotiating to do as it is.)

Several couples we know set aside time once a year for longer and more deliberate planning and dreaming. Our friends Ray and Gloria White Hammond, for example, conduct their strategy sessions of planning and intensive prayer as a couple in a carefully chosen spot away from home in January each year. Gloria reflects on how they

> think about what our prayer concerns are for the girls [their daughters],
> mentally, physically, spiritually, academically, and not only for them but
> for us, for our extended family, and our congregation. Then our various...
> activities, and local community stuff, and that has also been extremely help-
> ful because it helps us to focus and think about what we've got to do and

what things we need to just chip away and say no to. We don't do that perfectly, that's for sure; neither of us does. But it at least helps us to go back and say, *nah,* that wasn't fitting in the program.

This year their well-chosen strategy spot was Grand Cayman Island in the Caribbean. I know for a fact I would pray and plan very well on Grand Cayman.

It's ideal to get out of town, or at least out of the house, for a significant planning time, but finances or one spouse's lack of interest might not allow for this. Be as creative and intentional as you can. And of course, if Ray and Gloria would like to invite a group of us along to the Caribbean next January, I'm sure we could make arrangements.

Live on One Income—or as Close to It as You Possibly Can

Confession being good for the soul, let me hasten to add that although we've been careful to practice this as much as possible, there have been times when Todd and I have broken—smashed—our own rules in a desperate attempt to keep a roof over our kids' heads.

At times, the one-income goal can't be met, but if the whole system is set up—including what kind of house and vehicles purchased—to run only with two full incomes, then you're leaving yourselves very little room for layoffs, medical emergencies, or the possibility that one person might need more flexibility for children or an aging parent.

We've heard it before: the key is not to box ourselves in to having to work to pay for the toys we won't have time to enjoy if we have to work too much. And, just as importantly, living primarily on one income, when you've got two coming in, opens us up to all kinds of possibilities for other ways to direct those funds—like giving big chunks of it to causes that you as a family support.

And, lest we financially challenged types like me forget, there are also those lovely little details like saving for the kids' college education and our retirement funds.

Single parents all around us paddle their canoes by themselves, and even the possibility of this kind of thinking is several oceans of dreams away. And then there's a whole world of the barely surviving, who live and move and cradle their babies while famine reaps its daily harvest. It puts us to shame, those of us whose households offer the option of two incomes. We begin slipping and sliding down the hill of too many payments on too many Little Bit Bigger, Little Bit Nicer *things*. It's a trap. A trap we set for ourselves, often built of greed and self-focus. When the trap closes out options for us, we squawk in self-pity. I say this not as a self-righteous onlooker, but as one who's been there, one full leg in the clamp. Chew off your own paw if you have to and get yourself out. So you can number your days and accounts with an eye for what really matters.

Become an Organizational Giant

I am convinced that what we all learned about the birds and the bees and repro-duction is, in fact, bunk. Because some kind of funny business is going on after lights out in our house: Big Wheels getting together with Easy-Bake Ovens to give birth to more Happy Meal toys overnight.

Now, compared to other writers and professors, I'm not so unusual in my habits of tidiness and organization. The word *slovenly* comes to mind. In the past, I comforted myself that absent-mindedness was part of my job description as an English professor; a desk heavy-laden and groaning under mounds of half-read books and manuscripts in progress, I assured myself, was the mark of a writer. And the stacks of artwork and sports-team updates all over the kitchen? That was being a mom of very busy, very loved kids.

But the truth was that in my hands, millennia of human civilization were fast being undone, one unwritten thank-you note at a time.

Now, a better wife might've had compassion long ago on a husband always striving for neatness; a better wife might've reformed her pack-ratty ways sooner. But like any good recalcitrant sinner, I repented only when the sheer paperwork-weight of kids and career caused me to hit bottom, a new international low, and there was no other way out but back up. Because letting my worst qualities rule the days would mean that my kids would be left sobbing and permission slip-less in the school cafeteria while their friends boarded the bus for the NASA space cen-ter. And that all my students would have to get As—or all Fs—since their exams might or might not resurface.

Oddly, what has helped us more than any other one thing has been the addition of a third child. Her arrival sent our family over the brink from barely being able to find the bills when they were due and the dog when she needed vaccinating, all just before the onset of late payments and rabies, respectively, to a serious danger zone, complete with flashing lights and orange-striped barrels. Our flimsy organization system crashed, and we've begun to relearn better habits because we *have to.* And the *have to* has gradually been turning into a peculiar, unfamiliar *want to.*

Since this last move, we've gradually cleaned out each closet, labeled each square foot of each shelf, and invested a good portion of the family income in Rubbermaid drawers, also labeled, for each child to sort out toys and hobbies and art. And organizers for the adults divide the family's keep-on-file team rosters and class lists from the must-be-filled-out forms.

Dust, dog hair, and dirt I can bear and deal with as needed, since they're often attached in some way to creatures I love. But disorganization will be my life's ongoing battle. I sometimes picture myself in a twelve-step program for the organizationally challenged: *My name is Joy and I am a slob and it's been three days since I last left clutter on the kitchen counter.* I'm finding, though, that part of negotiating the three careers of our marriage means being intentional about keeping things organized—not because we need to feel guilt in the midst of capacity-plus schedules, but because organization helps create the desktop and the mental space we need to keep those schedules going and those permission slips actually turned in on time.

Beg, Borrow, and Steal Practical Timesaving Tips

It does seem to be a theme for those families in which the Big People work and the Shorter People are several: they've established clever timesaving systems to keep life rolling. Look and listen for others' ways of moving life forward efficiently and well. Assure friends or colleagues that imitation is the best form of flattery and unapologetically try out their system of tax-receipt filing or flip-flop shelving or sports equipment storage or chore allocation. If it fits with your family, keep it as yours.

Remember that even the little timesavers count; spare moments saved here and there can add up to more time to invest elsewhere. Because Pat Wilson (a law school professor) and her husband, Mike Jones (the director of environmental services for his city), not only both function in highly responsible professional positions and are raising two biological and several foster children at any given time, they employ a number of organizational shortcuts. For instance, they color-code everyone's linens in the house, so that if a green towel is left wadded on the floor, they know precisely who the culprit is—circumstantial evidence being plenty for this prosecution.

And here's the Pat Wilson–Mike Jones tip that has transformed my life: use a permanent marker to dot each family member's socks with his or her assigned color. And before being tossed in the dirty-clothes basket, all socks *must* be safety-pinned together by the wearer—or toe-looped in plastic rings made for this purpose. No unpaired socks will be washed. Dissenters can go barefoot for the rest of their natural lives.

The result? No more tedious hours of mindless sock matching. *Voilà!* Time enough on your hands for…who knows? Put on some Sinatra and a couple of candles and ask the person you married to dance. Remember to deadbolt the door.

Carry Out Chores with the Whole Crew—to a Good Beat

Much is still written about how the average dual-career couple does not dually share the housework: somehow women still end up with the brunt of the dust-bunny battles. Some analysts suggest that in couples where husband and wife work a similar number of hours, husbands do 45 percent of household chores;[5] some analysts suggest less.

When I asked one friend, Susan Matthews, a music teacher, about her take on the housework gender disparity, she mused a moment, then suggested that perhaps many couples face what she and her husband, Kyle, a songwriter, experienced: many women see the housework that needs to be done sooner than men see it at all. "Kyle has always, *always* been perfectly willing to do anything around the house I've asked him to," she said. "But I had to get past the feeling of 'I shouldn't have to ask, and you should be able to see for yourself what needs doing.'" The I-shouldn't-have-to-ask perspective turned out to be of no help to anyone. And, she reminded herself, her husband was willing to work hard at whatever needed doing. Mercy toward one another, she observed, was key. And learning to ask.

A good beat to work by also goes a long way in enlisting relatively cheerful child labor. In terms of music to mop by, we tend toward the bright, bouncy, and beach-focused. Jimmy Buffett, for example, relieves some of the pain of confronting the sink caked in red Spider-Man toothpaste.

Yes, a six-year-old *can* empty a dishwasher without breaking all your wedding stoneware. And if a bowl gets cracked now and then, isn't the trade-off worth it? Kids thrive on being given real jobs. And adults thrive on having the dishwasher emptied.

People who are more analytical than anyone in my house find chore charts or job wheels helpful. Todd and I just expect a lot of our kids. And when the planets are aligned correctly, they give a lot back.

When I asked one mother of seven how they survived at her house, she told me, "You'd be *amazed* how young children can do their own laundry." And that the minimum allowable age drops with each passing child.

Diana Garland, dean of the School of Social Work at her university and a mother of now-grown children, offered reassurance to those of us who function without chore charts: "We didn't have a lot of success assigning kids chores, but we kept at it. What was more successful was tackling chores together and making them a family activity. It took longer to go to the store with kids, to have them help, but it paid off in good time together."

Prioritize the Things Only You Can Do; Then Delegate

Vashti Murphy McKenzie stresses that she learned early on, "nobody really cares who does the housework, just as long as it gets done." She discovered that the things no one else could do—being there for her husband and her kids or scheduling utterly immovable weekly family nights—had to remain the priorities, whatever else had to slide or be hired out.

I must tell you that the people I interviewed fall into opposing camps on what to do about housework: to hire out or not to hire out. This is true even among those who could afford to do either.

A couple of minister friends of mine are both firm believers in housekeepers, and though their total family income is squarely middle class, they are tremendously busy and find that by throwing money at dust, dirt, and grime, they free up more important cracks and crevices of time. It makes sense.

Unfortunately, my husband and I are both products of Depression-raised parents, and find ourselves metabolically incapable of paying anyone to vacuum our floors.

"If we can't clean our own however-many square feet," my husband grouses to the mop, "we need fewer square feet."

But we happily take other shortcuts and let some multinational conglomerate chop our vegetables for us and freeze them and sell them to us in a bag we slice open above a hot skillet, along with the peanut sauce someone else packaged and offered on sale.

High on my own list of duties to be ditched—I mean delegated—would be cooking. Todd is the far more inspired chef in our house, while I've made my own culinary name among friends by having, at separate times, caught one cookbook, one cutting board, and several potholders on fire. But even so, I've learned to relish the squeals of delight over a particularly well-flipped banana-blueberry-walnut pancake—my own weekend specialty. And I love our long kitchen table being filled with our kids and their friends, all of them hungry and happy and loud. And expecting to be fed.

So I'm struck by the words of women like broadcast journalist Andria Hall or academic dean Diana Garland, who find that home cooking can be a kind of family cohesion. Here's Diana:

> I think the most important thing we did was that I cooked—a lot. We had supper together as a family virtually every evening and didn't let anything else interfere except in unusual circumstances. Of course, there were lots of squabbles and frustrations, but we were squabbling and frustrated together. There was something deeply important to me about feeding my family home-cooked meals that went beyond simple nutrition. It was communion.

All of us, though, must choose our own shortcuts. So consider, as the good Bishop Vashti instructs us, making a mental list of what *cannot* be cut—of what you and *only* you can provide. And take it from there.

Maximize Flexibility in Your Job

If you ever have a choice between more money and more flexibility and you're in the midst of raising kids, think *seriously* about choosing the latter.

National Public Radio's *Marketplace* recently aired a piece on blue-collar workers and the perils of balancing work and kids. Story after story depicted an unfair, unforgiving system: how those with the least flexible child care—often parents tag teaming—also work the least flexible hours. This means that one spouse who is suddenly slapped with mandatory overtime endangers either his own job or the job of his spouse. One worker's suggestion? That those in the decision-making echelons of management, often with premium day care or nannies themselves, eliminate mandatory overtime altogether and approach work-family issues with more compassion.

For those without management clout—and also those in professions known for long hours—it can be crucial to learn before accepting a job what the hours-per-week expectations will actually be.

Back in our one-child days, when we still held dinner parties, among the guests invited one evening were a female law student at Duke interning for the summer in a large, prestigious firm and a male attorney who was up for partner in the same firm. The law student, married and wanting to begin a family in the not-too-distant future, watched the clock as the attorney failed to arrive at the dinner from work. When at last he joined us, she was straightforward in letting him know that the firm had presented itself to her as family-friendly and wanting to attract capable women. Did he, she wanted to know, regularly keep these kinds of hours? I don't recall just how he responded. Perhaps she kept watching and kept asking questions of the other attorneys that summer and drew her own conclusions. What I do know is that she and her husband, also a lawyer, opened their own small firm together before starting a family.

Having an institution's expectations in writing can also be helpful, when appropriate. A former neighbor of mine, under pressure to spend more time at work (and less with her family), found it helpful that her initial contract stated particular expectations, which she'd faithfully met.

Since the time that I met Jane Tan in Cambridge, Massachusetts, when she was a young single woman with a drop-dead résumé, she has learned a great deal about drawing lines between work and home. Now the mother of two and a physician and Stanford University professor, she observes, "I put limits on what I will and will not do at work, and I made my boundaries and limitations clear with my superiors from the beginning. I make it a habit not to bring work home, and we are quite rigorous about having dinner together every day. If there is more work to be done, it has to wait until after the children are asleep."

For many of us, even our first summer job teaches us how earning a reputation as a hard and a valuable worker—or not—helps determine how much leeway we have in leaving work on time and still being respected as a team player.

Blowtorch the Television

If you're using the television as a chance to gather as a family and eat popcorn and drink hot chocolate and remember what it feels like to be curled up together like a litter of puppies, then television is a gift. If it's a diversion, though, from hearing about somebody's day or their dreams or their hopes or their hurts, or if it's time when you and your spouse could be packing the kids' lunches or going through backpacks or briefcases to make the next morning more calm, then hide the remote from yourself or put a chair leg through the screen.

We've heard all this before, in all those scolding the-American-Family-Is-Going-Down-the-Tubes kinds of articles. They just happen to be right in this case, along with watching our french-fry intake.

My middle-school daughter informs me our family is *totally* Iron Age for not having cable, not to mention the latest technology, whatever it's called, that makes cable look old-fashioned. It's probably true that we are deeply uncool. And quite frankly, we don't have HBO not because we don't like movies but because we like them so much. We're all pushovers for a great story, in a book or on a screen, and having so many lovely stories just a remote away would be too much for our tribe of weak souls to handle. So instead, we check out movies from the library for a family night with pizza. And during an overnight in a hotel, we channel surf till we don't know our own names anymore. You can see the evolutionary clock spin backward just watching our faces.

But television doesn't give shape to the day or fill in the cracks when the day has so few cracks in it to begin with.

Let Your Résumé Reflect *All* Your Work

If you or your spouse decide at some point to take time off from financially compensated work to stay home with children for a time, don't let yourself be intimidated by résumés without the same gap. And be conscious during this season of what you're doing or have done in a leadership capacity.

I once read an interview with Madeleine Albright in which she affirmed that she had never had a "real" job before the last of her three children went to school, although she served in any number of responsible volunteer positions. She suggested to the reporter that there ought to be some sort of system for evaluating the résumés of individuals who've taken time off work to stay home with children but who've meanwhile led groups or conducted fund-raisers or presided over boards. There's no national rating system for volunteerism, but you can still craft a résumé that includes all time spent in leadership, even if you weren't in a paid position.

Now, changing the 93,456 dirty diapers gets nobody any credit, no matter how well you word the thing: *Responsible for addressing hygiene requirements, particularly regarding fouled disposable infant-specific items and other refuse of all relevant parties...* But it does build character and a properly humbled sense of place in the universe. You might also want to keep in mind that all jobs in all fields have their elements of refuse disposal.

Keep Your Eyes Open for All Sources of Help in Your Field

A professor friend of mine in New England applied some years ago for a writing grant that would give her time to publish the book she'd been researching. When her paperwork reached the final round, it was clear that the handful of men among the finalists had published more than she had so far. She'd been working hard and steadily, but as the mother of special-needs kids, she'd been significantly slowed in her pace.

After considering all pieces of the applicants' personal and professional lives, the committee decided my friend showed the most potential and could most benefit from the career turbo-boost of more time to write: she was awarded the grant. The grant apparently existed for just such extra pushes to a stalled or slow-start career.

Some universities have set up significant grants for parents who are research scientists to hire lab assistants when someone simply has to be in the lab at 3:00 a.m. Some of these grants have also paid for nannies to assist professors when they attend out-of-country conferences to present their work. The grants, not surprisingly, have drawn fire from those without children and those who believe the money should be directed to those less educationally privileged. But it has undeniably led to many parents being able to proceed in their careers—finding-a-cure-for-cancer kinds of careers—who previously might have foundered on the shoals of competing goods: the infant who needs feeding at the same time the test tube needs checking.

Be Real-Estate Realistic

Unless you're a farmer or forest ranger—two jobs I could build real fantasies about—chances are that the houses nearest your work will cost a lot more than the ones with more acreage and more square footage and more whistles and bells far away from your work. Calculate the difference in time over the course of the year. Sure, you could listen to National Public Radio or learn a foreign language on tape as you drive back and forth to work. But you could also be spending more time with your kids.

For one-career families, a killer commute can be made to work, I suppose. Just this morning I heard a radio interview with a businessman who had a two-hour train ride to downtown Chicago *each way.* He was explaining how nice it was to get work done on the train, to have time to himself away from the kids. This is not someone who can spell his wife at the pediatrician's so she can get to her board meeting on time.

My husband and I made the dreaded distance mistake in China Spring, Texas, where we built a house well out of town. It was only twenty-five minutes from our jobs, we reasoned. With flat, fast roads and no notable traffic and no snowy days of impeded travel, how bad could that be? But we neglected to notice that the Barnes & Noble and Starbucks, our church, the doctors and grocery stores, the Home Depot and Tex-Mex restaurants and Target were *all* twenty-five minutes from our house. A once-a-day commute was, in fact, no big deal, but we rarely pulled off a day of only one trip. The roads were indeed fast—two-lane highways with a speed *limit* of seventy. *Two*-lane. Speed *limit*. Welcome to Texas. Everyone, of course, traveled much faster. It wasn't so bad when the kids were very little and would sleep during the commute, but when they grew into Bickering-in-the-Back-of-the-Car ages, we the Big People driving the cars grew fangs. Eventually we moved into town—walking distance from a favorite restaurant, a football stadium, a library, and a hardware store.

I still fantasize about living out in the country with horses. But given how far out of most cities the affordable horse property lies, I may have to wait for a season when we're not running kids and ourselves in a thousand different directions. That may be a season when I'm too old to relish mucking a stall anymore. But meanwhile, a girl can dream, can't she?

Develop Community with Other Parents Who Are Passionate About Their Callings

If possible, be intentional about finding parent-friend types who are passionate about their professional callings. Not that they need to be in the same season of life that you are or making exactly the same decisions about career and kids. But having a few people with whom you can exchange the occasional e-mail or meet for the occasional lunch can be hugely reassuring. It reinforces that you may not be a callous, cold-hearted ogre for missing aspects of your job while you're taking some time off for young children or that you may not be an undedicated worker because you're always planning how to work more days from home so you can be with your kids. And if in the unlikely event you have become the ogre you fear, you need friends who will tell you that, too.

The small group to which Todd and I belonged during the time we were deciding whether to bring a third child into our lives through adoption will always hold a velvet-roped corner in my heart. It wasn't just that these were people of about our ages who were also struggling with the idea of listening to God. It wasn't simply that they were all parents. And it wasn't merely that they were people who could offer a gripping, sometimes heart-wrenching *why* for what they did for a living. It was all of the above, in combination, so that none of us had to insist how much we adored our children or apologize that we enjoyed our work or explain that some days we weren't always entirely sure what God wanted from us, but that we were trying to hear.

Set Aside Regular Dates

Going out with your spouse once a week is ideal if you can afford it, but at some point baby-sitters began making more than plumbers. A once-a-week date at our house could mean not feeding at least one of the children or not fixing the pipes. Some people set once-every-other-week dates—just so it's a regular calendared event that you can look forward to and fend off all who would insist on your time. This includes adorable Small People who are stricken, threatened, and nauseous at the thought of Mommy and Daddy together alone.

When money is tight or the favored baby-sitters have all been abominably self-ish and accepted dates to the prom, we often create dates within family outings. One local restaurant brilliantly installed a small, fenced playground that sits just beside an outdoor dining area and charming pond. With the careful accumulation of coupons, the meal doesn't have to equal our paychecks, and this baby-sitter, the playground, doesn't have to be paid. Todd and I can often conduct an actual adult conversation while we wait for the food or the check as the offspring tire themselves out for an early bedtime. A DVD player and eighteen-inch television screen provide a home theater for us to actually enjoy that early bedtime.

However you choose to arrange it and fund it, reconnecting with your spouse and exchanging sentences that don't begin with one of your children's names would be the point. This is a tough one for me. But I do recognize what the marriage gurus tell us is true: much as we love and adore our kids and would give two eyes and an ear for them, our best gift to them can be the healthy relationship of their parents. This means, paradoxically, having conversations that don't always center on them. And conversations that do delve into the struggles and dreams of our professional lives.

Do Drudgery for the Glory of God—or at Least Try

I recently sent a hurried e-mail to a friend and former colleague in which I signed off that I needed to get back to writing and to the laundry that was taking over my house—but good thing Jesus didn't much care about laundry. This friend, Virginia, taught English part time on the university level until the addition of their fifth child. Her husband, Chris, teaches biology. *Why is it,* I thought to myself as I sent the e-mail, *the amount of laundry in life with children seems to compound daily while our savings account doesn't?*

But Virginia promptly responded, "I certainly hope Jesus cares about laundry, since I spend so much time doing it. I like to remember Brother Lawrence."

Point taken. In his little classic, *The Practice of the Presence of God,* Brother Lawrence writes of the grim rhythm of daily chores as an opportunity to focus on God.

As a child, I developed a violent allergy to some mysterious, blessed ingredient in scouring powder and have since clung to and nurtured this allergy, as it means my husband takes on cleaning bathrooms. And perhaps I'm still not spiritually morphed enough yet, but Soft Scrub rarely leads me to any metaphysical insights higher than wishing my son could learn to wash the sink out after brushing his teeth.

But in the chore of laundry, okay maybe *there* I can sometimes achieve something like the beginnings of at least God-ward focus. At least in folding the laundry, I'm thinking fond thoughts of each family member, provided they've remembered to turn their socks right side out, and I'm maybe remembering to pray for each as I go. I'm also often reminded of the privilege of owning more clothes than we need and of a washing machine that still holds together, despite all its groans to the contrary.

And for lots of us, including me and perhaps you, there's something strangely satisfying in DustBusting that neglected mantle or shelf—a visible sign of accomplishment that we can't always see in professional work. And even more rarely in parenting.

Carve Out Time for Family Conferences

If not every week, at least now and then set aside a meeting time to set the tone of the family, establish the principles you want to live by, define some family goals. It may be a good time to hand out allowance—or announce why, in some cases, it's being withheld—and discuss division of labor. And commend improvements, say, in a particular Small Person's manners.

Working families of all sorts are busy—too busy, of course, for one extra commitment. Except that this kind of heart strategizing as a family reminds everyone what you're about as a crew. It may even help highlight some outside commitments that can be let go because they no longer fit.

I particularly liked what Elizabeth Rogers offered as her family's effort at this:

> We brainstormed our "family values," coming up with just a list of words
> that we wanted to live by. We had butcher paper everywhere with markers
> and we all just wrote words off the top of our heads. Then we consolidated
> into themes and ended up with: CLORP, which stands for Compassion,
> Love, Order, Respect, and Peace. We painted together a large canvas with
> CLORP in the middle, which is posted in our kitchen. Then, we talked
> about acts we could all perform separately and together to help make
> CLORP a reality for our family…. We still talk about CLORP and can
> say that "word" to each other as a reminder of what we're about as a Christ-
> following family…. The main idea is that we involved everyone in the dis-
> cussion, and my kids always respond to being treated like people with valid
> ideas.

Weigh No One's Value by His or Her Income

This would seem to be an absolutely self-serving point for a writer and part-time professor to make. Writers and teachers and social workers and for-a-while-anyway-stay-at-home parents have no choice but to cling to this philosophy. But it also happens to be a good, moral, ethical, and spiritual principle.

A friend of mine in a fairly small city was recently being wooed by a job opportunity in Houston, where no doubt she would have been admired and adored—and, I'm certain, made more money than she is making now. But one of her two children has special needs, and the school where he was enrolled had helped him immensely. She and her husband decided they needed to stay put for the time being. It's gutsy to think this way: valuing family members according to what they contribute and where they are thriving, not just who brings in a whopping paycheck. Or not.

Waste No Energy Whining

I'm always hoping to find in the New Testament—or I'd settle for Garrison Keillor—some sort of official endorsement of whining. On my way this morning to a meeting at the college where I teach in Nashville, I slid into a good swamp of "poor me," feeling beat up by a comment of an extended family member and by deadlines and money stresses and a night of sleep lost to a baby's fitful tears. But the bottom line is that self-pity, good as it feels in the moment, drains energy and time, accomplishes nothing, and smears perfectly good mascara. So often I find myself thinking how much tougher women have it than men or parents have it than professionals without kids or writers have it than, say, fashion models, or adjunct professors have it than people who make actual money.

Writer Doris Betts allows no such sniveling, and I admire her all the more for it:

> Everybody has hindrances.... I could have been a woman with servants and a husband who made sure her writing came first, but Virginia Woolf still suffered from her own mental hindrances. There's always something. T. S. Eliot *can't* have enjoyed working in a bank.

I carry these words with me—and also mental pictures of blizzards in Boston. During all those New England winters, I learned a thing or two about parking on ice. I try to remember those winters, because whining is a little like spinning your wheels on thick ice. It doesn't do any good, and you wear out your tread in the process.

Never Lose Sight of Purpose

Do whatever you can to remember the purpose behind the life you and your family are leading. Speak of it to your kids. Listen well for the whispers and the thunder of the One who holds your mornings and your nights, even those that come too early and stretch too late.

Remember, this day is a gift. It may include a longish kiss from your spouse and big tourniquet hugs from your kids. It may bring with it learning, sometimes in the form of stiff winds or storms. It might bring good news, a goal or two stepped toward in your work.

For any of us, all these things can be a part of our purpose. Guided, when we're paying attention, by the One who is the beginning and end of all journeys.

Well Worth the Ride

My life was always
singing its way between joy and obligation.
—PABLO NERUDA

For those of us trying to pursue both meaningful professional and personal lives, on some days we feel like an updated version of The Little Engine That Could: chugging up the big hill, "I *think* I can, I *think* I can, I *think* I can," only to lose the grip on the track and begin the big slide, caboose first, back down the mountain, wheels screaming: "What was I *thi-i-i-i-i-inking!*"

The daily barrage of articles from the Mommy Wars would have us believe that this *is* a war, with one "side" emerging the winner. And that daddies are somehow exempt from the discussion and also from any potential disruption of calendars and career dreams. And that someday we'll know the answers to which side was right by how many children of two-career parents versus those with a permanent stay-at-home mom emerge as Heisman Trophy–winning neurosurgeons who practice medicine in a one-room clinic in Botswana, yet save well for retirement and fly home once a month to take their mothers out to dinner.

Granted, plenty of us struggle with guilt, stress, and frustration over how we can effectively juggle work and family. But our ways of thinking about commitments inside and outside the home can become polarized, as if enjoying work outside the home and loving one's family is a lose-lose battle. I've tried in this book to provide a different ideal—one that still includes a struggle for balance but *a struggle that itself is a privilege.*

Those of us who spend time thinking about how we might put to use talents or education or job skills can never lose sight of how fortunate—and unusual— we are. Taking that privilege seriously might mean taking the less comfortable road. Which just might make for an exciting, unforgettable use of a life.

The Burst of a Heart

Too many approaches to thinking about *just* career or *just* parenting or *just* marriage lead us to obsess over our own table settings and bedrooms and boardrooms and not of the tables that have no food on them. There's nothing wrong with a life that includes examining our own family's dental-care plan or our own career ladders, but there's also everything right with stretching our horizons into worlds where mothers lose their own teeth in their twenties and cradle babies who cry for food the mother doesn't have to give them.

Has parenting limited the number of hours I could spend on my professional life? Absolutely. But parenting, by connecting me with troubles outside my own, has also helped define my professional life. And my professional life—and that of my husband—has kept our kids and us connected to a world outside our own lovely bubble of manicured soccer fields and excellent medical care. For me, parenting has been a Grinch-like exercise in feeling my own heart grow to burst its tight metal box.

However Todd and I have failed as parents, I'm certain our children are becoming different people because they are functioning as part of our crew. They are confident of their parents' support at every ball game, recital, and budding interest, and they also provide their own loyal and loud response to their parents' efforts, including the conferences well conducted, the classes well taught, the book deadlines met—*and* the big, belly-flopping failures.

Even as I pound out this final chapter, the book's deadline looming, my precious co-parent seems to have come down with something—and he's rarely sick.

He's still insisting, though, on picking our youngest child up from preschool and working from home this afternoon so I can write. Tomorrow he's leading a conference, so I'll take the seat at the tiller to free him up. Sometime today and tomorrow, the kids will climb trees and fold clothes and do homework and practice piano and vacuum—most of it cheerfully, perhaps some if it not. And although there's no time for it, somewhere in there we will watch March Madness ball games—we have a dog in this fight and can't miss it.

Some weeks this kind of plan will go swimmingly, and some weeks Todd and I will wonder what we were thinking when, just yesterday, we congratulated each other on how smoothly our life was going and how shiny the kitchen floor was. It's inevitable that things will get messy again, the floors and the schedules, and that every so often someone will scowl and someone will sulk. It's highly unlikely—you can lay money on it—that any landscaping or living room of mine will ever appear in glossy, full-color fame painstakingly detailed by the *Better Homes and Gardens* crowd. And it's also a safe bet that I will not accomplish every last thing on my list I'd like to get done in a day, and that goes for the rest of my crew. But we'll get done what we need to, or most of it—together.

And together we'll keep helping one another watch for the winds of the Spirit, correct for mistakes, and steer some kind of good course between demands and delight.

Can't Doesn't Have to Define Us

Truly, there is reason to believe that the *can't* we hear all around us does not have to define who we are or how we try to navigate our lives.

Perhaps it's time we claimed hope in a culture that holds room for respecting the caregivers—whether of young children or aging parents or the sick and disabled among us—as well as the office-based workers.

I believe it's time to celebrate a world that allows room for women as well as men to wander the jungles of Honduras and the war-torn regions of the Sudan and the urban centers of Southeast Asia and lead stings of child-prostitution rings and help build orphanages for AIDS orphans and operate a grinding mill for former slave women to earn their own living.

It's time to admire, and emulate too, all those people around us whose ardent love for their own families and friends heightens their concern for the health, safety, and security of others worldwide and *their* loved ones.

It's time to applaud an era in which a man would put his professional goals and ambitions on the line for the woman he loves, just as she does for him.

It's time to sit up and take note when traditional gender roles get mixed up a bit so that everyone wins: men get to tuck babies in and watch them reach up with a smile of complete trust, and women get to have their ideas respected at the big conference tables with the nice views of the park. And our sons and our daughters can dream of their own futures without pink or blue borders.

It's time to appreciate a world where both women and men can not only speak candidly about the tensions between their personal and professional lives but also can point to ways in which their personal lives strengthen and guide their professional drives and how their professional passions, in many cases, have grown out of concerns for their own families.

It's time to trust in a God who leads us to risk and to push and to run...and to rest. To step out of the boat and never forget where our power and vision and sense of purpose come from.

It's time to participate in the possibilities of hope and peace and healing in the midst of the most desperate circumstances—and to believe in what immeasurable changes even one person, or one family, can make in our world.

It's time to take part not in the war we mommies are supposed to be waging but in the wisdom and encouragement and challenge we parents can be to one another and the ways we can move forward together, against wind and tide.

It's time to celebrate.

Questions for Discussion

Introduction: Mistakes Under Sail

1. Was there anything about how you and your spouse met or got engaged that held hints of your future life together?
2. Would you describe your own marriage as "smooth sailing"? Why or why not?

Chapter 1: Sailing and the Three-Career Marriage

1. Do you typically describe yourself as a "working" mom/dad or a "stay-at-home" mom/dad or something else? Do these terms fit or make you uncomfortable?
2. Do you ever find yourself defensive about your current season's choices in how you're navigating kids and career? If so, in what way?
3. The author observes, "Women are capable of so much good but also so much damage toward ourselves and one another.... Meanwhile the men struggle to march out as fully engaged fathers and fully supportive husbands and fully proficient professionals—a complex, multipart role they may never have seen modeled." How have you found this to be true in your own life?
4. What would you name as the immovable elements in your own working family? If you are reading this with your spouse, list your answers separately and then compare your lists.

Chapter 2: Against Wind and Tide

1. The author tells a story of a group of college students divided along gender lines. When have you observed or been a part of this kind of intense emotion and uncertainty regarding how to manage kids and career?

2. Do you feel as if your generation had good role models for crafting a healthy working family?

3. Has there been a particular point in your family life together that your system for handling personal and professional lives suddenly crashed? What was your response and that of your spouse?

4. How do your children respond to baby-sitters, day care, or other kinds of nonparental child care? How do you handle their responses?

5. In what ways, specifically, are you "making a difference" through your personal and/or professional life? Are there other ways you'd like to be doing so?

Chapter 3: Launching Out

1. What would you describe as the areas in which, to quote Frederick Buechner, "your deep gladness and the world's deep hunger meet"?

2. What are you *good* at? Is this at the heart of your professional life or do you wish that it could be?

3. How important is it to you to be passionate about your job right now? In what ways do you consider this a season of life when you and/or your spouse must think more in terms of simply paying the bills?

4. If money were not an issue, what would you get up and do every day? Is there any way to configure your family life (and income) to include more hours in the week for doing what you just named?

5. When you were a child or teenager, what did you tell people you wanted to be? Did you become that? Why or why not? How might you reclaim elements of those early dreams?

6. For you, how important is a spiritual dimension in thinking about the idea of calling?

Chapter 4: Spectators on Shore

1. Do you now or have you in the past struggled with criticism, either having it aimed at you or aiming it too often at others?

2. In what ways do you and your spouse differ in handling criticism?

3. Have there been junctures in your adult life when everyone seemed to want to weigh in on the decisions you were making? How did you handle this? Are there ways you wished you'd handled it differently?

4. For you and for your spouse, how important is it that your own parents think highly of your kids-and-career decisions? What sort of impact does this have?

5. How have you learned—or are you in the process of learning—to listen to God in this area?

Chapter 5: Charting the Course as You Go

1. Give an example of a friend or colleague's life that went an *entirely* different direction than they planned. Has any unexpected good grown out of that?

2. Are you someone who longs to plan out life ahead and likes a high level of control, or are you fine with just taking life as it comes? What about your spouse?

3. How has having kids been different from what you imagined ahead of time?

4. How might your career look different someday when your kids are older? What about your spouse's career?

Chapter 6: Loving the Big Wind

1. On a scale of 1 to 10 from Calm to Crazy, where would you place your life as a family?

2. Are you comfortable with the pace of your life right now? Is it more exhilarating or exhausting—or does that depend on the day?

3. What aspects of your schedules signal to you not just a nutty pace but also rich and full lives? What aspects signal the opposite—craziness without a sense of purpose?

Chapter 7: Avoiding the Shallows

1. What ways have you and your family learned to serve together? In what ways would you like to serve together more?
2. If this is a struggle, what are the biggest barriers?
3. What are some groups or other families with whom you and your family could serve—serving dinner or sorting clothing donations at a homeless shelter, for example?
4. How might your children participate, or even lead the way, in getting your family more involved in service?
5. Is there any particular thing or a certain direction you've long felt God was nudging you toward in terms of caring more actively or more generously for those who are hungry, destitute, forgotten, or without a family?

Chapter 8: Man—and Woman—Overboard

1. Has there been a time in your marriage you'd describe as a "hurricane season"? How would you summarize what happened?
2. In what ways have you "held the ropes" for a friend's or colleague's marriage in the past? If you haven't had that experience of direct support, talk about your observations of other marriages that have gone through rough seasons. How have your observations of others affected your own marriage?
3. The author refers to religious gatherings in which no one speaks openly or vulnerably about their own lives. How might we do a better job of creating spaces where people feel they can be honest about what is going poorly in their personal or professional lives?

Chapter 9: A Slowing-Down Season

1. How fast would you describe your family's pace of life in this particular season? How does this compare to a few years ago?
2. Have you reached points in your family life when things were clearly spinning out of control and something had to give? How did you

handle this? Or, if that point is now, what do you see as some possible solutions? Do you and your spouse agree on this or do you have different perspectives?

3. The author refers to several individuals who have used or are using time home with small children to strategize or rethink their careers. If you or your spouse were to take time off (or if you are currently taking time off) from the workplace, what things could you do to help keep you connected and growing professionally?

4. Has there ever been a time when your children "picketed" you as Andria Hall describes? What changes could you make in your family life and budgeting to allow flexibility if you find that you need to decrease professional hours in the future?

Chapter 10: Taking Turns at the Tiller

1. Have you or your spouse ever relocated for the other's career, or for one of you to go back to school, or for you to be closer to extended family? How did you make the decision as a family to move?

2. Have you, your spouse, or your kids ever had a difficult adjustment with a move? How did that affect your family as a whole? These days, an American family moves on average every five years. What are some concrete ways to help make the adjustment easier?

3. Taking into account both parents' careers and the kids' needs, what might be some good, healthy ways a family could approach considering whether or not to relocate?

Chapter 11: When Work Is Away from Home Port

1. Do you or your spouse travel for work-related reasons? How does the Home Front Spouse handle things while the other is away? What disaster stories do you have related to the Laws of the Traveling Spouse?

2. If you or your spouse have taken time off from work, and therefore travel less, how has that loss affected you personally and professionally?

3. What are fair expectations on the part of the Home Front Spouse when the Traveling Spouse returns? What are fair expectations on the part of the Traveling Spouse?

Chapter 12: Letting Go That Whale of a Goal

1. What things in your personal or professional life are pulling you under right now?
2. Give an example of when "letting go" in your personal or professional life had unexpected positive outcomes.
3. Are you someone who falls in the I-Can-Do-It-by-Myself category? Is your spouse? How do you handle this tendency in yourself or your spouse?
4. Of the Letting Go suggestions the author makes, what do you most wish you and your family could implement? What items would you add?

Chapter 13: All Hands on Deck

1. In what ways have you seen your kids benefit from having two parents who are passionate about their work?
2. In what ways do you see your family working together as a crew? In what ways do you wish you could work together better or more fully?
3. Describe the father-child relationships in the family you grew up in and now the one in which you're living. How do these differ?
4. The author names several ways in which our culture has learned important lessons by adapting to women in the workplace. Can you name others?

Chapter 14: Help for the Hopelessly Seasick

1. Of the "tools" the author offers, which ones might be particularly helpful to your family situation right now?
2. What would you add to this list that you've found helpful in keeping a three-career marriage moving forward?

3. If you were going to establish a new rhythm to your days, how would you go about doing so? Where would you start?

4. How does your family divide up the "grunt work" of life? In what ways could you do this better?

5. Make a list, as Vashti Murphy McKenzie suggests, of the things in your family life that only you can do. Now make a list of things only your spouse can do. Finally, make a list of things that could be delegated or hired out or simply left undone.

6. Given your own experience, what is your one best piece of advice for other working families?

Conclusion: Well Worth the Ride

1. List as many things as you can that are worth celebrating about your personal and professional lives and the ways these work together.

2. In the course of your busy life, which of these things might you forget to be grateful for?

3. What is the very best thing about the way your own family works together? What new, good things do you hope and pray for the future?

Notes

Chapter 2

1. Joan Hedrick, *Harriet Beecher Stowe: A Life* (New York: Oxford University Press, 1994), 138. Calvin Stowe is quoted in an 1840 letter to his wife.
2. Harriet Beecher Stowe to Sarah Buckingham Beecher, December 17, [1850], folder 94, Beecher-Stowe Collection, Arthur E. and Eliza Schlesinger Library on the History of Women in America, Radcliffe College, Cambridge, Massachusetts, as quoted in Hedrick, *Harriet Beecher Stowe*, 138.
3. Leslie Morgan Steiner, *Mommy Wars: Stay-at-Home and Career Moms Face Off on Their Choices, Their Lives, Their Families* (New York: Random House, 2006). *Mommy Wars* is one of many examples of books on this subject. Other women who have spoken out on this subject in much-cited books or essays in *New York Times Magazine, Atlantic,* and *New Yorker* include Caitlin Flanagan, Linda Hirshman, Sandra Tsing Loh, and Lisa Belkin.

Chapter 3

1. Frederick Buechner, *Wishful Thinking: A Seeker's ABC* (San Francisco: HarperSanFrancisco, 1993), 95.
2. Doris Betts, "Whispering Hope," *Shouts and Whispers: Twenty-One Writers Speak About Their Writing and Their Faith,* ed. Jennifer L. Holberg (Grand Rapids, MI: William B. Eerdmans, 2006). This O'Connor story was also confirmed for the author by Baylor University professor Ralph Wood, who once heard O'Connor herself tell it.
3. See Matthew 25:14–30.
4. Thomas Carlyle, *Past and Present,* (New York: William H. Colyer, 1843), 113.
5. United Nations Department of Economic and Social Affairs, Division for the Advancement of Women, www.un.org/womenwatch/daw/followup/session/presskit/fs1.htm.
6. See Luke 12:48, KJV.

7. Bruce Morgan, "The Healer," www.tufts.edu/home/feature/?p=white hammond. This online article was taken from the original version, which appeared in *Tufts Medicine,* summer 2004.

8. Bret Lott, "Toward Humility," *Fourth Genre* 1.2 (Fall 1999): 156–73.

9. T. S. Eliot, "Journey of the Magi," from Ariel Poems in *The Complete Poems and Plays, 1909–1950* (New York: Harcourt Brace Jovanovich, 1952), 68.

Chapter 4

1. Deborah Tannen, *You're Wearing THAT? Understanding Mothers and Daughters in Conversation* (New York: Random House, 2006).

2. From Peggy Wehmeyer's commencement address to Gordon College class of 2002, as reprinted in Gordon College's *Stillpoint,* (Summer 2002): 4–7.

Chapter 5

1. In a brief but personal chat with the Nobel laureate.

Chapter 7

1. Philippians 2:13.

Chapter 8

1. Ecclesiastes 4:12.

Chapter 9

1. Emily Bazelon, "The Swing Vote," *New York Times Book Review,* February 5, 2006, 21.

2. Lisa Belkin, "Her Morning Shift," *New York Times,* August 13, 2006, online edition, http://www.nytimes.com/2006/08/13/magazine/13viera.html?ei+ 5070&en+5fd59090aeef0.

Chapter 10

1. See Psalm 137:1–2, 4.

2. Psalm 121:1.

Chapter 12

1. Brennan Manning, *Ruthless Trust: The Ragamuffin's Path to God* (San Francisco: HarperSanFrancisco, 2002), 5.

Chapter 14

1. Dorothy Bass, *Receiving the Day: Christian Practices for Opening the Gift of Time* (San Francisco: Jossey-Bass, 2000), 116.
2. Bass, *Receiving the Day,* 23.
3. Jane Kenyon, "Otherwise," in *Otherwise: New and Selected Poems* (St. Paul: Graywolf Press, 1996), 214.
4. Dietrich Bonhoeffer, *Life Together* (Minneapolis: Augsburg Fortress, 1996), 92.
5. Kurt Sandholtz and others, *Beyond Juggling: Rebalancing Your Busy Life* (San Francisco: Berrett-Koehler Publishers, 2002), 17.

Conclusion

The epigraph for this chapter is taken from Pablo Neruda, *Fully Empowered,* trans. Alastair Reid (New York: Farrar, Straus and Giroux, 1975).

List of Personal Interviews

Doris Betts (writer and former professor at University of North Carolina, Chapel Hill), in e-mail correspondence with the author, October–December 2002.

Elaine Chao (United States Secretary of Labor), in a telephone interview with the author, December 16, 2002.

Shannon Sedgwick Davis (attorney and VP of Geneva Global), in e-mail correspondence and phone conversations with the author, September 2003–July 2006.

Diana Garland (dean of the School of Social Work, Baylor University), in an interview with the author in Waco, Texas, Spring 2003, and in e-mail correspondence, spring–summer 2006.

Jennifer Grant (dentist in private practice), in e-mail correspondence with the author, January 2006.

Andria Hall (broadcast journalist), in an interview with the author in Waco, Texas, November 13, 2002.

Ray Hammond (former surgeon, current AME pastor), in conversations with the author in Boston, Massachusetts, fall 1988–spring 2006.

Robin Hanna (founder, Signs of Love, based in Honduras), in an interview with the author in Waco, Texas, October 20, 2002.

Joe Kickasola (professor of communications, Baylor University, but based in New York City), in e-mail correspondence with the author, winter–summer 2006.

Linnea Kickasola (opera singer based in New York City), in e-mail correspondence with the author, winter–summer 2006.

Bruce Kuhn (actor, based in the Netherlands), in an interview with the author in Waco, Texas, September 15, 2003.

Susan Bahner Lancaster (professor of literature), in personal conversations and e-mail correspondence, spring–summer 2006.

Linda Livingstone (dean of business school, Pepperdine University), in personal conversation and a telephone interview with the author, fall 2002.

Mairead Corrigan Maguire (Nobel Peace Prize laureate), in a conversation with the author in Waco, Texas, October 29, 2003.

Vashti Murphy McKenzie (bishop, African Methodist Episcopal Church), in an interview with the author in Waco, Texas, February 17, 2003.

Thanne Moore (speech pathologist, Lexington, Kentucky), in e-mail correspondence with the author, January–February 2006.

Carole Pomilio (speech pathologist in Phoenix Arizona), in e-mail correspondence with the author, January–March 2006.

Elizabeth Rogers (computer specialist, Belmont University), in e-mail and personal correspondence with the author January–February 2006.

Kelly Shushok (minister of small groups, Calvary Baptist Church, Waco, Texas), in e-mail correspondence and telephone conversations with the author, fall 2003–summer 2006.

Jane Tan (physician and professor, Stanford University), in e-mail correspondence, summer 2006.

Sally Weaver (physician and assistant professor through University of Texas Southwestern Medical School, Dallas), in e-mail correspondence with the author, January–February 2006.

Peggy Wehmeyer Woods (host of World Vision Radio), in an interview with the author in Waco, Texas, fall 2003, and in telephone conversations, July 2006.

Gloria White-Hammond (pediatrician and minister, Boston), in a telephone interview, fall 2002,and in conversations in Boston, Massachusetts, fall 1988–spring 2006.

Betty Williams (Nobel Peace Prize laureate), in a conversation en route to Dallas, April 17, 2000. Although the author does not quote Williams in this book, the Nobel laureate's insights were instructive and helpful to the author's grappling with this subject.

Patricia Wilson (law school professor), in e-mail correspondence with the author, March 2006.

Karla Worley (singer and writer), in an interview and subsequent conversations with the author in Franklin, Tennessee, winter 2006.

About the Author

Joy Jordan-Lake, PhD, is the author of *Grit and Grace: Portraits of a Woman's Life* (Harold Shaw Publishers, 1995), *Whitewashing Uncle Tom's Cabin: Nineteenth-Century Women Writers Respond to Stowe* (Vanderbilt University Press, 2005), and a book forthcoming from Paraclete Press. A former Baptist chaplain at Harvard University, she has also served as the associate pastor of a multiethnic church in Cambridge, Massachusetts, where she headed compassion ministries with homeless and low-income women and families. She has been a primary editor for *Christian Reflection,* an ethics journal, and a speaker at retreats, conferences, and seminars.

Currently an adjunct professor at Belmont University in Nashville, Tennessee, she has taught writing and literature at Tufts University in Medford, Massachusetts; Eastern Nazarene College in Quincy, Massachusetts; Wingate University in Wingate, North Carolina; and Baylor University in Waco, Texas. Joy and her husband, Todd Lake, are the parents of three children: Julia, Justin, and Jasmine.

Joy is an enthusiastic advocate for domestic and international adoption and for microenterprise loans that help individuals in impoverished, unindustrialized countries begin their own businesses in order to support their families.